T0063096

THE CALL

RESPONDING TO THE CALL

Dr. Milicent J. Coburn

Order this book online at www.trafford.com
or email orders@trafford.com

Most Trafford titles are also available at major online book retailers.

Printed in the United States of America.

ISBN: 978-1-4907-1842-2 (sc)
ISBN: 978-1-4907-1844-6 (hc)
ISBN: 978-1-4907-1843-9 (e)

Library of Congress Control Number: 2013919578

Trafford rev. 02/13/2014

 www.trafford.com

North America & international
toll-free: 1 888 232 4444 (USA & Canada)
fax: 812 355 4082

TABLE OF CONTENTS

ACKNOWLEDGEMENT

I want to thank the many who supported and strengthened me along my journey. Your prayers and well wishes are deeply appreciated.

DEDICATION

Dedicated

To the memory of my late parents Mr. and Mrs. Joseph Coburn,
for their unconditional love and excellent parenting.
I will always cherish the wonderful memories.

To

Bishop Courtney H. Williams, Sr.
First Lady Merna Elaine Williams
Mrs. Aleece Angus

and

Reverend Pleasant McGowan
Who were of tremendous assistance to me in
assembling the material for this book.

To

My former administrator Mrs. Edna Somers
and her assistant Mrs. Daphne Mason.

Also To

Rev. Cynthia Salmon   Doteriez Edwards
Lilleth Campbell   Carmen Cohen
Thelma Greig   Ruth McEnnis

ABOUT THE AUTHOR

D r. Milicent J. Coburn was born in Pleasant View, St. Andrew, Jamaica, West Indies. She is the daughter of the late Joseph and Vera Coburn, and the eleventh of twelve children. She is the mother of two adults.

Dr. Coburn attended elementary school and St. Joseph Teachers' College in Jamaica. She was an elementary school teacher in Jamaica for many years, prior to migrating to the United States of America. She relocated from New York to Connecticut, where she currently resides. Dr. Coburn worked in various areas of employment, including Nurses' Aide, Home Health Aide and Early Childhood Education. She had a vision of becoming a Child Psychologist but someone dissuaded her. She did the prerequisite for nursing school, but returned to the passion of her life-teaching.

In order to fulfill her vision of becoming a public school teacher, she was vigilant about attending schools of higher learning. She attended the Housatonic Community College and graduated with a Certificate and an Associate Degree in Early Childhood Education. She studied at the University of Bridgeport, where she received a Bachelor's Degree; Southern Connecticut State University where she received a Master's Degree. She did a second Master's Degree and a Doctorate in Christian Education, at Biblical Life College and Seminary.

Currently she is a kindergarten teacher at a Bridgeport Public School. Dr. Coburn attends Refuge Temple Church of God in Bridgeport, Connecticut, where she is a very active member. She teaches Sunday school, serves on the Mothers' Board, and is a volunteer of the Shelter Ministry, where she assists in preparing meals for the homeless.

ABOUT THE EDITOR

Jean Murray is a born again Christian and was a property manager for many years.

Jean enjoys writing and has successfully edited published works. She is currently working on her first book of poetry.

As an editor, Jean has the ability to weave the author's "hidden spark" into the flow of the work; thereby capturing the reader's interest from start to finish. Due to her keen sense of attention to details, Jean ensures that the sequence of events move the content along. This is her hallmark approach to editing. As a poet and songwriter, Jean brings freshness and perspective to editing in a unique manner.

Jean resides in Connecticut, USA with her husband Paul.

INTRODUCTION

I am amazed and fascinated by the variety of calls that each person experiences and makes during his or her lifetime. We are all bombarded by calls, and yet I realize that we cannot exist without them. The Webster Dictionary gives many meanings to the word "call", but I prefer:

> 1. "announce or proclaim; attract the attention of; rouse from sleep; and to bid, as by divine command."

Some calls can be urgent, and then there are those that have to be placed on "hold". Some calls are detrimental, while there are others that are frivolous and intrusive.

Yes, there are calls, but I think the most important of them all is the call from God that may mean life or death. It needs special attention. People respond to calls in numerous ways . . . .

Aay, long time since nuh hear your voice
Before we talk let's pray
Don't call back this number
Hello
Hi mom
How did you get my number?
I am not home
I am not ready, Lord
I can't speak Lord
I'll pray for you first
I was thinking about you
I will report you to the governor
It is you again
Leave a message and I'll call you
Lord, I am not worthy

Lord if you . . . .
　　　Lord I'm but a child
Lord I'm too young
　　　Lord, I will . . . .
No more money
　　　Not home
Not now, Lord
　　　Please hold
Remember that Jesus loves you
　　　Same number you just called, he/she
　　　is not here
Sorry, this is it
　　　Thank you for calling
Try this number
　　　We are not home; leave a message and
　　　we will call you back
When I get married, Lord
　　　Who are You Lord?
Why are you calling me now?
　　　You are going to live long
You have the wrong number
　　　You know

From a biblical point of view, God began the Call way back in the book of Genesis. He did not require an answer, because he knew what the response would be. God requires man to be honest. He is so loving and compassionate that He did not leave man isolated. God created Adam and at the designated time of the day when it was cool and relaxing, He would go and visit with Adam. God was such a good father and a special friend to Adam that he would not allow Adam to seek him, but instead He visited Adam. One day when God made his regular visit, Adam was nowhere to be "found". God then initiated His first call to the man:

"Adam where are you?"
Genesis 3:9 (NLT)

God has made many other calls to man since his first call. He calls the rich and the poor, the young and the old, the renown and the unnoticed. God called in the olden days and continues to call.

God calls in mysterious ways, for example, Hagar received an amazing call for one main reason, she was a woman and that was unusual. The angel visited her and ministered to her in a unique manner. It reminds me that God calls whomever he wishes regardless of one's status. He meets everyone at his or her lowest ebb. God calls men as well as women because he called a disrespectful, insubordinate maid. He called her to supply her needs and to inform her of the future of her son.

God called unto Moses out of the midst of a burning bush and Moses responded. Samuel was called and he did not realize that God was calling him until Eli the Priest explained that it was God who was calling him.

The calls continue to bombard us daily and we make excuses or we may respond positively. We may meet the needs of others at the moment or we may delay doing so. We sometimes postpone our response and in the end we forget to do so, and lose out on a blessing, that we regret for the duration of our life. Calls can be pleasant, interesting, burdensome, kind, caring, loving, intrusive, painful and informative. No matter the form in which the calls come, they cannot be prevented and for our entire life we will receive calls and make calls.

FOREWORD

This book is very interesting and informative on a wide spectrum of issues. It takes us back to the very beginning of mankind, down through the annals of time to the present time.

The book is aptly titled *The Call*, as it emphasizes the importance of and the various types of "Calls". From the first man Adam being called after the fall, down to and including the single most important call of our life, that of course is the need for us to answer affirmatively to our Savior's call. Both the individual who is very adept with the scriptures and the person who is trying to find his or her way, will be enlightened and fulfilled by the contents of this book. Dr. Coburn gives us suggestions for a purpose-driven life without dictating to us, thereby allowing us as Christ has allowed us, to make and follow our own conviction.

In my role as a financial planner, I am privileged to travel and meet hundreds of individuals every year, to help formulate, review and implement financial strategies. The spiritual principles and examples given throughout this book, will undoubtedly assist me in my practice as I pursue prayerfully, never forgetting God in my daily life and not only searching for Him in times of crises. Let me hasten to say that these spiritual principles and practices are universally applicable regardless of one's vocation. Therefore, if due care is given in searching the wisdom contained in this book, it will positively impact your life and general affairs.

I thought that I had a good collection of stories, Bible stories and others, but Dr. Coburn uncovered far more than I thought possible. She also reminded me of events that I had long forgotten. Her wonderful collection of stories do far more than just making the book interesting. They give me a better understanding of our storied past and a greater appreciation of the struggles our spiritual forefathers endured in paving the way for the freedom we enjoy today. In addition, this book redirects our focus back to our Creator and reminds us of our duty to faithfully serve Him.

Congratulation, Dr. Milicent Coburn, on hitting the right combination of spiritual principles, historical events and storytelling. Although simply stated, the book is inspiringly powerful.

Norman S. Leslie, ChFC, CASL, LUTCF

CHAPTER ONE

THE PERSONAL CALL

Reaction to parent's call

A call is unique because it can be verbal or nonverbal. A nonverbal call is understood by the person to whom it is directed.

Reward or Punishment

Result of Positive Response

Parents have devised ways to call their children, verbally and non-verbally. A child who responds to the parents' call in a positive manner will be rewarded with positive reward. Some parents train their children through nonverbal communication, by the look of their eyes or by the direction of a finger, and in each case the well-trained child will respond. These children constantly look at their parents for the next instruction, and although others who are in close proximity do not hear words, the child interprets the message and responds.

Result of Negative Response

Children who do not respond in a positive manner when the parents call, will be punished. The punishment can be physical, verbal, or valued time or object may be withheld or taken away permanently. Children who want to avoid punishment try to respond in the proper manner.

Babies Call and Parents Identify the Call

Babies are very perceptive although they are young; they are able to identify their mothers from a group of people. They will call by crying, by looking around while making little sounds, or even by reaching out their little arms and kicking their legs. The crying of a baby has meaning to a very caring mother. She knows if that cry means that the baby is hungry, wet, soiled, sick or just needs some attention.

A mother will sometimes look at her baby and walk away because she knows that the child is just crying for attention. She is sometimes wrong because her conclusion may not be so, the baby may be ill and she does not detect that illness.

The Immediacy of the Call

Parents especially mothers, know their babies so well that they know how urgent the call is. Yes there are parents who withhold love and affection from their children, but there are others who respond as their babies cry. Some babies just want to be held, so when the parents pick them up, and cuddle them, they feel happy, and relaxed. Babies cry and they say to the parents, "I need you now. Leave everything and come to me." They need their call to be answered and without delay. The babies are so self-centered but they do not know it, for they have no name for their action. Some of these babies develop to be selfish young people because of the attention that they received by their crying, they now use it to manipulate their parents.

CHAPTER TWO

THE SOCIAL CALL

Visitation

People sometimes drop by the homes of friends and relatives without warning, and or notice. They just arrive at the destination that they choose, and the visits can be from a few minutes to days, a year or more. It is strange to have someone visiting, who carries a number of pieces of luggage. Some of these visitors will use a statement as "I was in the area, so I am just dropping by."

A short visit can sometimes be as burdensome as a long one, and it all depends on the person who is visiting. A troublemaker's short visit may cause the one visited to tell a lie, or make an excuse about having an errand to run. I heard of a story about a woman who was doing her laundry by hand when an undesirable visitor showed up. She did not want to have a conversation, so she filled her mouth with some of the dirty laundry water. She was preventing herself from participating in a conversation with someone who could not be trusted or is a slanderer.

Neighbors in rural areas of some countries call upon each other in a different manner. Some ladies would 'drop by' or send a child to the neighbor who lives a far distance away to borrow some sugar or other food items. The sugar may be measured in a mug (cup), so the repayment of the loan would be precise. Many city folks are not aware of this practice because they reside very close to the supermarkets, but the country folks sometimes live half-a-mile from the shops. Neighbors are not embarrassed to borrow food items. They live very far from each other, unlike the people of the suburbs, and in the large cities, they depend upon each other.

Friendly Telephone Call

How pleasant it is to pick up the receiver and listen to a cheerful voice on the other end of the line informing you that he or she was just thinking about you. The caller may say that you just came into his or her thought and he or she makes the call. It may be that they got an urge to call you or God laid you upon their mind so they make the call.

The call may come at a time when you are experiencing some difficult circumstances. I remember times when I needed to hear from another individual because I felt alone, and God allowed someone from another state or another country to call me. Friendly calls can be very informative. We may be missing out on an announcement when someone calls to keep us informed. We sometimes receive invitations by telephone calls, and these may include summons to the movies, a shopping trip, a luncheon, to dinner, to attend church services, to go for a walk, or to meet someone you have never met. A friendly telephone call is like a glass of cold water that a thirsty person receives. We are happy to receive calls that are not overbearing or calls that cause us to regret that we answered the telephone. Modern technology has afforded us the privilege of filtering our calls. We have telephones that announce the telephone number of the incoming call and that enable us to refrain from accepting that particular call. We also have caller identification and other equipment that identify the origin of the call.

Courting Call

One day I visited a farm and observed a buck trying to get the attention of a doe, so he was prancing and spitting and was really acting crazily just to woo the female. We were warned by one of the keepers that we should not interrupt him, so we just watched as he performed in pain. I cannot say how successful he was because I left the area before he got a reply from the female.

Some of our men court in the same manner as the buck, with one exception, they do not spit. They will follow a female around and in some cases they actually stalk her just to have a relationship. Women are no different from men in these modern days; they also target men and become aggressive in order to have a date. The real man knows how to talk when he is courting, even if he is deceptive. He has the right words that will melt the heart of an angel. He has the right words to say. Girls and women who have been hurt in previous relationships sometimes feel comfortable with the promises that this "Don Juan" gives, only to realize later that that man was really a "Player." Courting can be very unpredictable because many of the promises go without fulfillment.

Women make promises during the courting call, and they themselves lie to the men. The ladies know how to dress, talk, walk, smile, and smell to give the men false security, and then later they hurt them. During courting, both men and women are liable to hurt each other with the words they speak, and the commitments that they make.

The courting call can be very effective and can cause both persons of the opposite sex to be swept off their feet. The call can leave a savory taste in the mouth of both persons that will cause them to lose their sleep, and also forget their meals. When these two persons of the opposite sex are courting, time passes on without them realizing it. The correct words, the look, the voice, and the caring, cause the ones who are courting to ignore and forget the world around them. The courting call is an emotional period when adrenaline runs high. The parties find it difficult to hang up the receiver. They have a difficult time saying goodbye. The persons who are involved are almost inseparable even if they do not reside in the same town or country.

Bird Call/Imitating the Bird's Call

Bird call can be made for several reasons. A mother bird may be about with her brood and she identifies a hawk or predator lurking overhead, so she then summons her chicks to safety. She makes a chirpy sound that informs the chicks that danger is near and those chickens understand and run for shelter under her lifted wings. There may be one chicken who lingers longer than the others and the mother makes a sound so that that wandering chick escapes the impending danger. After the chickens are safe and secure, the hen hovers over her brood and makes certain that not even their little heads are exposed to danger.

Birds cry or call to other birds for a time of friendship. They sometimes preen themselves and others when they assemble together. They communicate to each other in languages that the human being cannot fathom. I read an account of one of the slaves whose father took her to the woods to listen to the various calls of birds. He taught her how to identify danger through listening to the birds. She identified feelings of those birds just by listening to their song. Men have developed bugles and other instruments to imitate birds in order to trap them. Musical instruments are used to imitate the high notes that birds can produce.

The rooster is a phenomenal bird. Those birds can get the attention of their peers. They even have crowing matches to prove who the master is. Roosters on one farm can compete with others on another farm to inform them that they are the masters in that area. They will compete in such a way that the others will finally give up on crowing. Some roosters try to claim certain territory by crowing and just by chance, if a young rooster is on that farm, the older one would challenge him in a fight.

Roosters call families to arise and get to work. I lived in the country where there was one transistor radio and a clock in the home. Everyday someone had to wind that clock, but I was not sure how accurate it was. The rooster on the other hand consistently aroused the family, especially my father, at approximately 5:00 a. m. As soon as the rooster crowed, there was stirring in the home; and although we glanced at the clock, the rooster was the most reliable time-teller.

One morning that rooster crowed and my mother got up, woke my younger brother and me to assist her with her produce to take to the market. Mom and these two smallest, sleepy, children were out of the house, on our way to join a lady to get to the bus. Mom discovered that the rooster had fooled her, and it was in the dead of night, but decided that she was going to proceed to the other lady's house. Ms. Napier was asleep when we arrived at her home, so we ended up sleeping on the floor until day break, when we continued on our journey.

We were upset but, could not express how we felt. Later we were able to come to the conclusion that the rooster was probably hungry when he crowed that night. People in the country still appreciate the rooster for waking them, although it is sometimes very annoying. Roosters are like kings on their own turf, and no one can keep them quiet. People do imitate them, but only the true rooster can crow.

CHAPTER THREE

THE PROFESSIONAL CALL

The Urgency of the 911 Call

In the United States of America, 911 is very significant. Its purpose is for someone to acquire assistance in an emergency. There have been cases where inconsiderate people use the 911 number for foolishness. Someone called to report that her order at the fast food restaurant was not what she had requested. There have been other silly calls as well. When someone who does not have an emergency calls, the system is tied up while those who are in imminent danger are neglected.

The 911 operators are expected to send assistance to those who are in danger. However, recently we heard of two children who were in danger, the social worker was on the telephone and the operator did not respond in the proper manner. This resulted in the murder of those children. The case-worker explained the danger that she thought the children were in, and the operator kept explaining that the call should be of life or death circumstance. No one can be sure that the lives of the children would have been spared, however, prompt assistance was necessary.

Children are encouraged to call 911 if there is a problem in their homes. Little children have been known to call 911 when their parents' lives have been in danger. Children as young as three years old have called 911 because their parents were unresponsive. Little children should call for assistance when one parent is abusing the other, because the child and the abused parent are in danger of losing their lives.

I was in an accident and called 911, their question was if I required an ambulance, because I declined, I had to wait more than half an hour. I called repeatedly and was informed that the police was summoned, and were on their way. I observed other people who had to wait in the middle of the street for the police who were not in view, just because no one was dying. I would not like to see someone in a remote area alone in her or his car waiting for the police. It can be just as dangerous waiting for the police.

There are teenagers and children as young as four years of age living in America who threaten their parents if they are about to spank them. I recall a case that I heard of. The adopted father informed his daughter, whom he parented from before the age of two, to pack her suitcase before she made the call; she did not call. Some parents are scared of punishing their children because they threaten to make a 911 call. I would rather suffer punishment, than allow my child to grow without correction. Parents should not abuse their children, but they should not neglect to scold them and allow them to grow into little unruly people. If the parents do not discipline rude children, then one day the police may have to discipline them.

911 has been very beneficial to many people whose lives have been saved. I think that improvements can be made to procedures for responses to calls, but the service is necessary. We are very grateful to have that service. Thank you 911 operators for the countless lives that have been saved; and the babies that have been delivered. 911 operators remain on the line and coach a scared father or someone in delivering a baby who decided not to wait to get to the hospital. When there is a sign of danger, and when in life and death situation, just dial 911.

The Demand of the Army Call

"Uncle Sam", (USA), is always in need of good men and women who will enlist in the armed forces. Representatives of the Selective Services are always seeking to enlist qualified men and women who are willing to obey "Uncle Sam".

The Selective Services which include the Army, offer incentives to attract those who will respond to the offer. There was a time when young men especially, were drafted in the army and if they resisted the draft, they could be imprisoned.

Some young people get enlisted because they plan to attend college at a later time and they think that a career in the army will give them a better opportunity to achieve their goal. It is sad to say that some of these veterans have served, but there is little hope in the civilian life for them. Some of them are walking aimlessly without a future after having served their country.

There are families who have lost their loved ones to "friendly fire," and in combat. Many veterans have committed suicide, and there are countless others who are suffering from one ailment or the other. Some veterans especially men are unable to cope in the society. Yes, there are others whose wives or girlfriends have taken their substance and sent them 'Dear John' letters. Many veterans have no observable scar yet they are wounded emotionally and it is impossible to predict if or when they will be healed.

Jury Call and its Execution

Citizens are minding their own business, and suddenly they receive a letter informing them to show up for jury duty. This is a call that cannot be ignored, no one can take this call lightly or else he or she may end up being incarcerated.

Those persons who send out the letters sometimes send them to the deceased. I do not know how they would respond if the deceased persons showed up for duty with their death certificates as proof that they are dead.

There are many of us who detest going to jury duty, and there are others who love it with a passion. I really think that the opportunity should be given to the ones who want to do that civic duty. A system is in place for the selected candidates to dial a number and listen for their names from a very long list of prospective jurors. By listening to those names you will know if you are to show up or not. Those candidates who are chosen have to be excused from their work for that day, and if they are selected to be on a case, then they will be away from their occupation for several days. The call to jury duty has no reward and there should be another method to select jurors. Those who have a love for it should be given every chance to go and serve their country.

The Job Interview and the Result

There are many of us who like to work for an honest living, and we place applications in different areas of interest in order to gain employment. We show up for the interview looking attractive, not too dressed and certainly not looking tacky. We want our prospective employers to see us properly attired to show how we will represent their company. We may dress down if we get the position, but for now we follow the advisors who inform the men to wear a tie and ladies to wear a navy blue suit.

Some of us might have been habitual late comers, very tardy, but we are early for the interview. We realize that we are in competition, not for American Idol or Miss World, but for a job. We desire employment and we are as someone says, 'Putting our best foot forward.' We make an effort to appear confident, so we walk properly when we are called and sit when we are offered a seat, and yes, we do not forget to be polite before we sit. We sit as if we were born sitting upright, with our hands on our lap.

At the end of the interview we are advised to wait for a call, and in some cases the call never comes. We may be the fortunate ones who receive the anticipated call. I think the prospective employer should get a glimpse of our reaction as that telephone rings and we pick up the receiver. Well, the call may simply state that "I'm sorry, but you have not been considered, so we wish you luck in finding another position." "You mean that after all that preparation, that effort, that interest, they turn us down?" It has happened to the best of us, and it continues to happen, we lose a chance to show how dedicated we are or how unreliable we can be. The call that informs us that we are chosen can cause the level of our adrenaline to elevate quickly. We sometimes feel tightness in our chest, so that the thank you comes out in a manner that we cannot explain.

I remember sending out applications to several prospective employers and received no response, but the Lord showed me the final position. When I called the woman asked me if I could attend the interview the following day because she was about to go on vacation, I acquiesced. After the interview she gave me a tour of the building and introduced me to some of the employees who were present. I was wondering why she was taking me around the building so soon, then she inquired, "Would you like the job?" I was so happy, I answered in the affirmative. I know that God had opened that door for me. I later learnt that she could not get people to work in that facility, so she was happy to take a good employee who had passion at first sight. I worked there for four years.

People are still applying for jobs, going on interviews, and listening for that anticipated telephone call. The call may bear good news and it may carry disappointing news as well. We continue preparing resumes and portfolios, for that dreaded day of the interview because we earnestly desire the job.

The Importance of Roll Call for Attendance and Accountability

I am almost certain that schools around the world have roll call. When the roll is called the teacher is afforded the opportunity to discover those who are present and those who are absent. The teacher who marks the names of those who are present is responsible to know the where about of those children for the duration of the school-day. He or she is bound to make sure that those who are present are safe.

When a child is missing from the class, the teacher should be able to state exactly where the child is to be found. In case of an emergency, for instance, a fire drill, the teacher should count all the children he or she has, to determine if someone is missing. It is easy for a young child to wander off into the bathroom, so the teacher should be aware of this situation. The roll call also affords the teacher the chance to keep a record of the truants and call home after some absences or report the absences to the proper authorities for them to check on the welfare of the child or children who are absent. The roll call can save lives in some cases, because officers will be called in to check on certain children especially those who reside in an unsafe environment.

The roll call is significant in that those children who are present when the attendance is taken are in good stead for perfect attendance at the end of the marking period. The children who are tardy with excuse are really present, but they were late. Taking attendance at the start of school is very vital.

I am not sure how roll call is done in prison but from watching certain movies, I noticed that the roll is taken. All the prisoners have to be accounted for. It does not make sense when there is a report that prisoners escaped and have been on the run for days before someone discovers that they are missing.

There is a different method of taking attendance at work, if someone does not report to work and did not call in, then he or she is marked absent. That worker is in trouble unless he or she went to the hospital with an emergency. It may be that there is serious trouble at that employee's home so he or she is absent. Dependable employees have set a standard that once they are absent for a day or two someone at their place of business will detect that there is probably trouble, and will alert someone to check on those employees.

Doctors' offices call patients to remind them that they have an appointment on a certain day, and at a specific time. The patients who have appointments sign in when they arrive and names are checked.

Some civic meetings have roll call of the names of the officers. The officers have a responsibility to be present; if they will be absent, they should submit a letter stating that they are unable to attend.

The airport has a system that makes an announcement for certain passengers. The public address system will announce the name of that individual and gives him or her proper instruction that he or she needs for a specific flight.

Some families have an informal roll call; parents, especially those with more than one child are always calling the names of their children. In some homes parents have to call four or more children when it is time for bed, a meal, to run errand, for school, and to attend church.

We are accustomed to so many roll calls in our life time here on earth, that one writer thinks we will have a roll call in heaven so he penned this song:

[2] When the trumpet of the Lord shall sound,
And time shall be no more,
And the morning breaks, eternal, bright
and fair.....

CHAPTER FOUR

THE SECRET CALL

David Spangler's Call

David Spangler's book, The Call, explains that when one receives a Holy call, it is a disclosure that comes from inside, it may just be a vision that makes the person take his or her attention from himself or herself and becomes a servant of the divine. Those people who are acquainted with us, including our family, will be intimidated by the change of the individual and try to reclaim him or her. David tries to explain what the call is:

> [3] "I believe that for many of us, when we think of the call and of being called, we are actually thinking of being summoned. When you are summoned, there is implicit in this idea a sense of direction. I am summoned to do something or to go somewhere specific. I am summoned to dinner. I am summoned to my work. I am summoned to the courthouse. I get a summons!

> A call, however, need not be that specific. It need not offer a definite sense of vocation or direction. In fact, some of the most powerful calls that we may receive in our lives, the calls that come from the deepest places in ourselves, are not summonings but are more like awakenings. They call us to attention.

> How often we have the experience of somebody calling our name and immediately

our attention is heightened. We say, "Yes?" or, "Here I am!" or whatever response is appropriate. The call may not carry with it any kind of implicit direction. The person doing the calling may simply want to know if we're here. For example, my youngest boy gets home from school. He comes in the door, and he calls out, "Mom? Dad?" He knows we're there, but he wants to be reassured that we're there. So from wherever I am in the house, I call out in response and let him know where I am and what I am doing, usually something like, "I'm over here. I'm at my computer, writing." (Someday I'd like to call out, "I'm lying on the sofa, eating sinfully rich mint chocolates and watching television!") The call may not be doing anything other than establishing a presence, determining that we're really here, that we've "shown up," as anthropologist and spiritual teacher Angeles Arrien would say. So the call may not be to a specific duty, but to an awareness of what the moment asks of us. It is a call to pay attention."

David gives an account of an occurrence that took place when he was a teenager. He accompanied his parents to see a movie that was called 'A Man Called Peter,' and this was really a life story of Peter Marshall, who was the chaplain of the United States Senate for some years. The film showed that Peter who was Scottish was travelling across the moors very late one night during a storm and reaching the edge of a cliff he heard a voice instructing him to stop. He could not see where he was going because it was very dark, he obeyed the voice, and stopped. The storm ended and to his amazement, he noticed that he was at the edge of a cliff, and if he had not obeyed that voice he would have fallen to his death. He felt that God had called him.

David had spoken to many ministers who revealed to him that God had called them to become ministers. Peter was called in the same manner just as other ministers are called.

It was a few years later that David had his own calling to choose another vocation from the one that he was pursuing. The film about Peter assisted David to prepare himself for his new position in life. David's setting was different from that of Peter's but he had a decision to make.

David was in college, and walking through his dormitory when he heard the call. David had to make a choice. He was in his third year, studying for his Bachelor of Science degree in biochemistry, with the intention of becoming a genetic engineer, but that soon changed. David stated that he was not going to leave college. This took place when the Vietnam War was raging, and he had had a draft deferment. David continues:

[4] "However, the inner worlds had another path in mind for me. They said, "Time for you to leave school." I said, "No."

I've always felt quite free to say no to the inner worlds, but they feel equally free to say no back to me if it seems necessary. Apparently, this time it was necessary. So about a week after I said no, I literally felt as if somebody had thrown a switch and turned my mind off. I went to class as usual, but now nothing the instructor said made sense. Nothing that I read made sense. It was like I had had a lobotomy. For a couple of months, I watched my grades plummet, until finally the penny dropped and I thought, *I don't think I'm supposed to be here. I'm supposed to be somewhere else.* So I left the university."

The call remained with David for years. He faced times when he was perplexed, but kept reminding himself that he was called. When doubt arose in David, and he questioned himself of who he was, he had to remind himself that the spirit had called him.

The Help Call

Carole Mayhall prayed frequently to her Lord, and she would always ask her heavenly Father not to allow her talk to go further than her walk. She and her husband Jack were associated with The Navigators for many years, and they both cared for the needs of others. This dear couple had a granddaughter who had an accident that cracked both the large and small bones in her lower leg. This five year old child could only watch other children enjoy themselves as they moved around while she was on crutches.

Sunny's mother was not able to take her through the streets and plaza to enable her to shop as her class was doing. The little girl was frustrated, so she was crying on her mother's shoulder:

> [5.] "Sunny looked pathetically at her mother and whimpered, "My *life* hurts more than my leg!"

> Sunny's perspective lament reflects the aching of many hearts. We take in stride the single pain of an area in our lives that begins to hurt. But when an avalanche of problems slams down the mountain to bury us, trapping us helplessly beneath, we cry plaintively, "Lord, my *life* hurts!"

> Yet God controls the avalanche. It can be His way to deliberately, methodically strip away that which will hinder us from knowing Him deeply. The force of an avalanche strips away supports we've counted on, often leaving us with nothing. Nothing, that is, but God Himself. The divine axe has fallen.

> Blow by horrible blow, I watch as the support limbs of my friend's life are hacked away.

Whack! And her effervescent mother lies dying and wasted.

Womp! And her own health deteriorates into chronic back problems and then diabetes.

Wham! And her lovely unmarried daughter gives birth to a baby to raise in her parents' home—a baby yellowed with jaundice, bruised—who almost doesn't make it through the first week.

Crash! And debts pile high from doctor and hospital bills, the plight of a mother, daughter, and grandson without insurance.

Whop! Bam! Whish! Irritations escalate, doubts rise high, things break, rest is nonexistent, and life becomes a nightmare of pain and frustration. Before my eyes I see my friend stripped to the bare bones of her trust as the divine axe falls again and again.

She's reeling from the blows. Numb and bewildered. I watch and cry." Carole stated that Max Lucado has written,

> 'The rubber of faith meets the road of reality under hardship . . . the trueness of one's belief is revealed in pain. Genuineness and character are unveiled in misfortune. Faith is at its best, not in three-piece suits on Sunday mornings or at VBS on summer days, but at hospital bed-sides, cancer wards, and cemeteries.'

My friend has experienced this literally. Her faith is meeting the road to reality this very minute. The bumps and potholes jar her, the twists and turns confuse her, the seeming endlessness of the journey leaves her baffled."

Carole stated that when God strips a person he or she may sometimes ask the question of what he or she did to deserve such treatment. She also asked if God had cast off the one who was suffering. She doubted the trust that the sufferer had placed in God. Was it useless?

The problems that Carole has been alluding to are constant, arriving one after the other. They come continuously without any break. Those situations are God's tests that He uses on His children to encourage them to forsake all their other props and rely on Him totally.

Carole and her husband were experiencing trouble, real agonizing stripping. They lost their jobs, relationships, their ministry, friendships, and their good name. They were going through harsh persecution. Carole terms what they were undergoing, as going through the fog or being placed in a prison without doors or windows. Carole implored with God each day for a job. It continued for two months, until God moved in her heart and reminded her to give Him thanks instead of getting so anxious. She cried for help, and confessed to God. She had to admit that she was anxious and He gave her peace for two months, He gave her the job of His choice. Carole quotes:

[6.] "In *Rose from Brier*, Amy Carmichael wrote,

"He shall choose our inheritance for us." I remember with what delight I found in *Young's Analytical Concordance* that the verb in this verse is the same as that used to show David's choosing, out of the possible stones in the brook, the five best for his purpose.

- 21 -

So does our heavenly David, our Beloved,
choose out of all possible circumstances (and
they are all at His command) the best for the
fulfillment of His purpose.

Perhaps one of His best "stones" is the fog,
blinding us to the army of God behind us,
the enemy Goliath in front of us, or the
triune God who is with us.

A couple of years ago, I wrote:
Father
    I don't like this!
        Mist has fogged all certainty.
I can't see!
There are no colors,
Not even black and white.
Just . . . gray.
    No clear-cut outlines,
    No vision of purpose
        or plans.
Just cold, wet mist

I'm terrified, lost, feeling abandoned.
But within my heart I know that,
    though I can't see You,
    Your eye is on me.
    Your hand holds mine . . .
        even though its touch
        is lost to me right now.

And from somewhere comes the
    knowledge that my
    quest for humility—

Your desire for my humility—
The mist is part of the path.

Not knowing,
        not understanding,
        not seeing,
are tools—important ones—
for teaching me . . . Well,
        as yet I know not what.

The mist diffuses Your Light—
        walls it back to me,
        confuses the source of that Light.
I'm unable even to look down
        to see the Rock beneath my feet.

I can only stand still
        and wait
        and listen
        and hope."

Ms. Mayhall quoted from Oswald Chambers: God called Jesus to what seemed like a calamity, and Jesus called His disciples to watch Him being put to death. Their hearts were torn to pieces as they watched Him, and it seemed to them that He had failed them. God knew that Jesus' death was not a failure because God's purpose was fulfilled in Him. God now calls us and does not state to us clearly what the journey will entail.

No one hears when God calls us, but we hear Him. What happens to us after He calls us is His prerogative; He is working out His intention.

7. "God's call to us is often baffling. What God calls "good" looks anything but good from our point of view. Who could call years of pain and seeming uselessness "good"?

But when God's call looks baffling to us that is the time we must *determine* to trust Him . . . to call on His grace to be sufficient for us.

The stripping from pain and helplessness is, in the hands of God, a tool of consequence and one not used indiscriminately. He does not trust the majority of us with this kind of life. Many of those He does call are crushed by the stampede of constant pain, weakness, and incapacitation. But those who come forth in victory—ah, those are the ones whose faith has been tried as gold. They come through the fire shining, their faith burnished, glowing, and pure.

Had an extra-special room been prepared for him when God said, "Welcome home, child" to Rev. Blackwell?

I'm sure of it."

My Call

I knew a wealthy man who had an extremely large property in my village. He resided in Kingston, but he hired men to care for his property. He purchased some cows and placed them in one area of his property. I am uncertain if the cows disliked the area, but unfortunately they dropped dead, one or sometimes two at a time. All the cows died.

The last Saturday night of May 1965, I dreamt that I was standing on the property facing a family plot on the opposite side. While standing in the pasture, I noticed someone standing in the family plot holding a long white shroud. Then I heard a voice calling "Grace, are you ready?" I was smart enough to know that the Lord would remove me from this earth if I did not commit my life to Him. I remember informing my friend, a teacher about my dream. She responded that she wished God would kill me. She did not mean it in a cruel manner; she just wanted to scare me into giving my heart to the Lord. I got baptized the following Sunday, June 6, 1965. I still recall the Hymn that they sang when I was going down the steps of the pool,

> "Now I belong to Jesus,
> Jesus belongs to me,
> Not for the years of time alone
> But for Eternity."

I am now ready in case my Lord comes for me in the Rapture or in death.

CHAPTER FIVE

THE URGENCY OF GOD'S CALL TO

Adam

Adam, God's first child had a loving, caring affectionate Father who visited him daily. Adam and his wife Eve lacked nothing; they both had the Garden of Eden to themselves. They lived in utter peace and security. Adam had control over every living thing that was on earth. He was not afraid of lions, poisonous snakes, crocodiles, or poison ivy. Adam and his wife were safe from all evil.

Adam was never hungry or thirsty. Adam and his beautiful wife had it all. They did not owe the telephone company neither did they have a mortgage. They did not know the word "foreclosure", yes, Adam and Eve had bliss on earth, that no one else who came after them will ever experience.

The Lord visited Adam and his wife Eve daily as a true, reliable friend would do. God gave Adam instructions and the only limitation Adam had was to leave the tree in the midst of the Garden alone. The Lord told them what the consequence of eating of the fruit from the tree that was in the middle of the Garden would be, it would surely result in death.

One day Adam was missing from his post, he left his wife alone for some time, and so she had a subtle visitor. The visitor was Satan, in the form of a serpent and he conversed with Eve about the trees that they were to eat from. Eve then remembered the forbidden tree that was in the midst of the Garden and she explained to the serpent that God instructed them to refrain from eating of that fruit. When Satan was informed that if they ate of the "Tree of Good and Evil" they would die, he told Eve that she should not trust God. The serpent twisted the words of God and made Eve believe that their Friend, God had deceived them.

Eve believed the serpent's lies that they would not die. He informed her that their eyes would be illuminated and they would be like their Creator. Eve bought into the lies of Satan and ate of the Tree, then she went and instructed her husband to do the same.

Adam forgot what God had told him and he obeyed his wife, who had gotten her instruction from the serpent. As soon as they disobeyed their Creator, they realized that they were naked, so they tried to cover themselves with fig leaves.

The wonderful, regular Visitor of Adam and Eve came for His constant visit, and Adam was missing from his post. The Lord had made Adam and Eve in His likeness, so He had constant companionship with them. Adam and Eve resembled God and they had His breath of life. Adam and Eve could not associate with the animals because they did not look like each other. God loved His children very dearly, so He came for fellowship, they could not be found, and they did not look the same:

> [8.] Toward evening they heard the LORD God walking about in the garden, so they hid themselves among the trees.
>
> [9.] The LORD God called Adam, "Where are you?"
>
> [10.] He replied, "I heard you, so I hid. I was afraid because I was naked."
>
> [11.] "Who told you that you were naked?" the LORD God asked. "Have you eaten the fruit I commanded you not to eat?"

[12.] "Yes," Adam admitted, "but it was the woman you gave me who brought me the fruit, and I ate it."

[13.] Then the LORD God asked the woman, "How could you do such a thing?"
"The serpent tricked me," she replied. "That's why I ate it." Genesis 3:8-13 (NLT)

Adam sinned, so he hid himself from someone who enjoyed fellowship with him. He fell by the serpent's trickery. Adam never enjoyed life since the day he sinned. He died spiritually, and lost Paradise.

Abraham

The LORD appeared to Abram one day and gave him a promise. He told Abram that He would make him a great nation. Abram was to leave his country, and his people, including his father, and his relatives and go to a land that he would receive. God did not show Abram the land, but God expected Abram to obey Him:

> 2. "I will cause you to become the father of a great nation. I will bless you and make you famous, and I will make you a blessing to others.
>
> 3. I will bless those who bless you and curse those who curse you. All the families of the earth will be blessed through you." Genesis 12: 2-3 (NLT)

I can just imagine that Abram's dad saw him packing and asked him where he was going and when Abram informed him that the Lord told him to leave, his father probably thought that his son was losing his mind. This heathen man could not believe that his son was going to leave because God called him, he did not really know God as we do.

Abram's father, Terah, asked Abram of his destination. Abram told him that he did not know the location, but that he was going. Abram's friends and relatives tried to reason with him, by explaining to him that he should not leave because it did not make sense. Abram could not be deterred, so he got his wife Sarai, his nephew Lot, and his servants and left Ur of the Chaldees to a land that he knew not.

Abram was a faithful man, to give up all his comfort to go for something that he could not see. He was a man of faith or rather "The Father of Faith." He believed in God and, so he obeyed God. God changed his name and the promised was fulfilled.

Moses

There was a goodly child, born in the house of Levi, whose name was Moses. Although Moses had two older siblings, Miriam and Aaron, he was marked for death. The king of Egypt had ordered the midwives to murder all the baby boys, but Moses was spared because of the action of his mom who prepared a little boat, placed baby Moses in it, and placed that little vessel in the river. She somehow believed that he would be safe there.

Moses' sister stayed close by and watched the little vessel. One day the daughter of the king, who had ordered the baby boys to be murdered discovered him in the river, and adopted him as her very own baby. Fate would have it that the baby's mother was employed to care for him as the first surrogate mother. Moses grew up as a prince in Egypt.

By and by Moses observed the Jews who were slaves then, being treated harshly. His mother had acquainted him with his real family, so when he saw the oppression of his people, his heart moved with compassion, and he ended up murdering one of the Egyptians who was abusing a Hebrew slave. The following day that same Hebrew man who was rescued, was fighting one of his fellows, and Moses intervened. The ungrateful man published the hidden story of Moses killing the Egyptian, and threatened Moses. Moses had to flee for his life because what he did made the king angry.

Moses abdicated the palace for the wilderness. Pharaoh, who loved Moses dearly, would have killed him if he had not escaped from Egypt. Moses fled to Midian, where God blessed him with a family. God trained Moses for forty years, and prepared him to lead His people in a very peculiar manner.

One day Moses was in the desert guarding his father-in-law's sheep when he observed a strange occurrence, a bush was burning, but it was not consumed. Moses was fascinated, so he stood by and gazed at the bush. He suddenly heard a voice from the bush and he heard his name.

4. So when the LORD saw that he turned aside to look, God called to him from the midst of the bush and said, "Moses, Moses!" And he said, "Here I am."

5. Then He said, "Do not draw near this place. Take your sandals off your feet, for the place where you stand is holy ground."

6. Moreover He said, "I *am* the God of your father—the God of Abraham, the God of Isaac, and the God of Jacob." And Moses hid his face, for he was afraid to look upon God.

7. And the LORD said: "I have surely seen the oppression of My people who *are* in Egypt, and have heard their cry because of their taskmasters, for I know their sorrows.

8. "So I have come down to deliver them out of the hand of the Egyptians, and to bring them up from that land to a good and large land flowing with milk and honey, to the place of the Canaanites and the Hittites and the Amorites and the Perizzites and the Hivites and the Jebusites.

9. "Now therefore, behold, the cry of the children of Israel has come to Me, and I have also seen the oppression with which the Egyptians oppress them."

¹⁰ "Come now, therefore, and I will send you
to Pharaoh that you may bring My people,
the children of Israel, out of Egypt." Exodus
3:4-10 (NKJV)

Moses had a dynamic call; his call is different from all the others. God
sent Moses to return to where he escaped from, to deliver those people
from the tyrant, Pharaoh.

Joshua

Moses led the Israelites and his era was up, but he had an excellent assistant by the name of Joshua. This man was very faithful, but I do not think that he had an interest in leading so great a nation as the children of Israel who had just come out of captivity. God called Joshua in a unique way and gave him a charge:

² "Now that my servant Moses is dead, you must lead my people across the Jordan River into the land I am giving them.

³ I promise you what I promised Moses: 'Everywhere you go, you will be on land I have given you—

⁴ from the Negev Desert in the south to the Lebanon mountains in the north, from the Euphrates River on the east to the Mediterranean Sea on the west, and all the land of the Hittites.'

⁵ No one will be able to stand their ground against you as long as you live. For I will be with you as long as I was with Moses. I will not fail you or abandon you.

⁶ "Be strong and courageous, for you will lead my people to possess all the land I swore to give their ancestors.

⁷ Be strong and very courageous. Obey all the laws Moses gave you. Do not turn away from them, and you will be successful in everything you do.

[8] Study this Book of the Law continually. Meditate on it day and night so you may be sure to obey all that is written in it. Only then will you succeed.

[9] I command you—be strong and courageous! Do not be afraid or discouraged. For the LORD your God is with you wherever you go." Joshua 1:2-9 (NLT)

God called Joshua in a way like no-one else, and gave him the responsibility of leading His people after the passing of Moses. Joshua was young, but reliable; he was faithful to Moses, now he became the chosen leader.

Samuel

Elkanah had two wives (which was legal in those days) Hannah and Peninnah. Hannah was barren, but Peninnah was so fertile, she gave birth constantly, and she mocked Hannah because she could not bear a child. Needless to say Hannah was very unhappy, and although her husband loved her more than Peninnah, that did not fulfill her desire, she pined over giving birth to her own child.

One day Hannah went to the temple and poured out her heart to the Lord. She promised Him that if He only gave her a male child, she would lend him back to Him. She was unselfish so she would willingly give back her child to the One who answered her prayer, by giving her a baby. While Hannah was praying with her lips only moving, but no audible words, the Priest, Eli thought she was drunk and rebuked her. She informed him of her heart's desire, and that she was not drunk. Eli gave her his blessing.

In time God gave Hannah her heart's desire and she gave birth to a boy whom she named "Samuel". Hannah weaned her son and with the permission of her husband, she took him to the temple and gave him to the Lord. When she gave the baby to Eli, she reminded him that the prayer that she was praying was answered and fulfilled in that baby.

Young Samuel grew up in the temple and was serving the Lord. Now Eli had two ungodly sons who disrespected the Lord and the people of God. Their father Eli did not rebuke them, so they did as they pleased. They made the Lord very angry because when the leaders cautioned them, they did not heed the warning, they got worse.

Samuel did not know the Lord, but he served Him faithfully; and there was going to be an imminent change. One night Samuel had the opportunity to know the Lord and that experience lasted for his entire lifetime. Samuel, the boy was asleep near the Ark of God, in the tabernacle, one glorious night:

⁴ Suddenly, the LORD called out, "Samuel! Samuel!" "Yes?" Samuel replied. "What is it?"

⁵ He jumped up and ran to Eli. "Here I am. What do you need?" "I didn't call you," Eli replied. "Go on back to bed." So he did.

⁶ Then the LORD called out again, "Samuel!" Again Samuel jumped up and ran to Eli. "Here I am," he said. "What do you need?" "I didn't call you, my son," Eli said. "Go on back to bed."

⁷ Samuel did not yet know the LORD because he had never had a message from the LORD before.

⁸ So now the LORD called a third time, and once more Samuel jumped up and ran to Eli. "Here I am," he said. "What do you need?" Then Eli realized it was the LORD who was calling the boy.

⁹ So he said to Samuel, "Go and lie down again, and if someone calls again, say, 'Yes, LORD, your servant is listening.'" So Samuel went back to bed.

¹⁰ And the LORD came and called as before, "Samuel! Samuel!" And Samuel replied, "Yes, your servant is listening." 1 Samuel 3:4-10 (NLT)

God revealed to young Samuel what he was about to do to the sons of Eli because of their sins, and utter disrespect for God Himself. God had Samuel's ears and attention for his entire life. Samuel was devoted to God, and he pleased the Lord.

Jonah

Jonah is probably one of the first Minor Prophets. He was the son of Amittai, and he was well aware of the pressure the Assyrians had placed on the people of Israel. These Assyrians kept invading Israel and on one occasion they had murdered Jonah's loving father. Jonah could not forgive those heathen for what they did to his family and nation. He had a grudge and the only cure was to see the oppressors destroyed.

Because of God's compassion, He decided to warn Nineveh prior to destroying it, so He chose none other than Jonah to warn that city of its impending judgement:

> [1] Now the word of the LORD came to Jonah the son of Amittai, saying,
>
> [2] "Arise, go to Nineveh, that great city, and cry out against it; for their wickedness has come up before Me." Jonah 1:1-2 (NKJV)

After the Lord spoke to Jonah, he got up, but not in response to God's command, he had his own agenda; he was running away from God to another area. Jonah boarded a ship to go on a cruise, and disregarded God's instruction.

After paying his passage, he went to the lower level of the ship so that no one would bother him, not even God. Jonah forgot that God's eyes see everything and so he could not hide from Him. While they were en route to Tarshish, there was a storm on the sea and the lives of all who were on board the ship were in imminent danger. The men began to throw their cargo overboard to lighten the ship, but nothing changed, so they started taking inventory of those on board and discovered the disobedient prophet sleeping in the midst of the peril.

The men woke up Jonah and asked him to give an oral resume. Jonah disclosed to them that he was a Hebrew running from his God, the God of all the earth. He then requested a terrible favor that they throw him overboard, because he was afraid of committing suicide. The men did not relish the idea of throwing Jonah overboard, but they decided to acquiesce.

Before complying they inquired about Jonah's background, and he informed them that he was a Hebrew, belonging to the God who made heaven and earth. The men gave their lives to the Lord, Jonah's God. Jonah thought that he would drown, but God is a merciful God, so he sent a whale, the first submarine, to pick up Jonah. Jonah was in the whale's belly for three days and three nights, he then repented and prayed to God to give him a second chance and spare his life. Jonah prayed earnestly and God caused the whale to travel close to shore and spit Jonah out.

Jonah now escaped the storm and the sea but he had no desire to warn the people of Nineveh. He was prejudiced, still selfish, and most of all he was disobedient.

> [1] Then the LORD spoke to Jonah a second time:

> [2] "Get up and go to the great city of Nineveh, and deliver the message of judgement I have given you." Jonah 3:1-2 (NLT)

Jonah discovered that the Lord did not play games, so he went into the city of Nineveh. It was a three day journey. Jonah warned the people, he shouted to them that their city would be destroyed in forty days if they did not repent. The heathen believed God and the king of Nineveh led his people to repentance. The king instructed a prayer and fasting that included all animals, children, and adults. God spared the city because of their humility and obedience; Jonah was the only one who was angry.

Jeremiah

Jeremiah's call was unparalleled to all other prophets, although Moses spoke back to the Lord. The Lord and Jeremiah had a dialogue; Jeremiah was subdued by the Lord's comment. We observe where God responded to Jeremiah, but Jeremiah's comments did not come directly from his lips to us, and because we are aware of the fact that God knows all things even the secret intents of our hearts; He knew Jeremiah's heart:

> [4] Then the word of the LORD came to me, saying:
>
> [5] "Before I formed you in the womb I knew you;
> Before you were born I sanctified you;
> I ordained you a prophet to the nations."
>
> [6] Then said I: "Ah, Lord GOD! Behold, I cannot speak, for I *am* a youth."
>
> [7] But the LORD said to me: "Do not say, 'I *am* a youth,' For you shall go to all to whom I send you,
> And whatever I command you, you shall speak.
>
> [8] Do not be afraid of their faces, For I *am* with you to deliver you," says the LORD.
>
> [9] Then the LORD put forth His hand and touched my mouth, and the LORD said to me: "Behold, I have put My words in your mouth.
>
> [10] See, I have this day set you over the nations and over the kingdoms, To root out and to pull down, To destroy and to throw down To build and to plant." Jeremiah 1:4-10(NKJV)

God had a mission for Jeremiah and although Jeremiah thought that he was incapable of performing that task, the Lord equipped him and sent him. Jeremiah forgot that it was God who gave people mouths and if He desired them to use their mouth, He would cause them to comply. Jeremiah's excuse did not stand against God's desire. Jeremiah's hands were too short to fight with the Creator of mankind. God knew that Jeremiah was the one He intended to use for that task, so He explained to Jeremiah that He knew more about him than he knew about himself. Jeremiah surrendered and became a mighty prophet indeed.

CHAPTER SIX

JESUS CALLS AND CONTINUES TO CALL

The Disciples

Jesus began His ministry, and He found Himself in the land of Zebulun and Nephtali preaching. He travelled to Galilee where He observed Gentiles who were in darkness and He preached to them. He instructed the Gentiles to turn away from their sins and turn to God. Jesus told them about the Light that was shining in the darkness where they were residing. These who did not know Jesus were to become acquainted with Him:

> [18] One day as Jesus was walking along the shore beside the Sea of Galilee, he saw two brothers—Simon, also called Peter, and Andrew—fishing with a net, for they were commercial fishermen.

> [19] Jesus called out to them, "Come, be my disciples, and I will show you how to fish for people!"

> [20] And they left their nets at once and went with him.

> [21] A little farther up the shore he saw two other brothers, James and John, sitting in a boat with their father, Zebedee, mending their nets. And he called them to come, too.

22 They immediately followed him, leaving the boat and their father behind. Matthew 4:18-22 (NLT).

Jesus knew that He had to build up His kingdom here on earth, He also knew that He needed people to assist, so He called these men who called others to assist with the message of salvation. Jesus lived on earth for about thirty three years and the latter three of those years were spent training these followers and meeting the needs of people as He traveled along the way. Jesus could do ministry alone, but it was important to involve others. It would have been tragic if Jesus did all that alone, then there would be no followers and no one would take up the baton. Thank God that Jesus called those men, who called others and now we in the twenty first century are still calling others, in varied manner and fashion.

Zacchaeus

Jesus' name had spread abroad, His fame was known throughout the region, and wherever He went crowds thronged Him. One day Jesus passed through Jericho, and a certain man named Zacchaeus, who was a chief tax collector, heard that He was in town, and he wanted to behold Him.

Zacchaeus was short in stature, and it was impossible for him to observe Jesus because a large crowd had surrounded Him. This man Zacchaeus devised a plan, he ran ahead of the crowd, and seeing a sycamore tree, he climbed it and waited for Jesus to pass by. He was at an advantage over many of the other people because he was having an aerial view:

> [5] And when Jesus came to the place, He looked up and saw him, and said to him, "Zacchaeus, make haste and come down, for today I must stay at your house."

> [6] So he made haste and came down, and received Him joyfully.

> [7] But when they saw it, they all complained, saying, "He has gone to be a guest with a man who is a sinner."

> [8] Then Zacchaeus stood and said to the Lord, "Look, Lord, I give half of my goods to the poor; and if I have taken anything from anyone by false accusation, I restore fourfold."

> [9] And Jesus said to him, "Today salvation has come to this house, because he also is a son of Abraham;

[10] for the Son of Man has come to seek and to save that which was lost" Luke 19:5-10 (NKJV).

I believe that Jesus went to that area of Jericho to bring Zacchaeus into the kingdom of God. All the others followed for what Jesus could do, but that man Zacchaeus wanted to see Jesus so that he could have his own testimony of Him. He was rewarded that very day and he in turn decided to make restitution when he received a changed heart. Those who were observing began to criticize as we would do, but Jesus forgave that man and made him a child of God. Zacchaeus was not the same since that day, he was a changed man.

Lazarus

Jesus had a set of friends in Bethany who had constant fellowship with Him. There were two sisters, Mary and Martha, and their brother, Lazarus whom Jesus loved dearly. It so happened that Lazarus got sick, and his sisters sent for Jesus. When Jesus heard that His friend was sick He remarked that it would not end in death, but would rather bring glory to God.

Jesus loved this family, but He remained at the location where He was for two days. He and His disciples had a discourse, after which He told them that Lazarus, His friend was asleep, and He was going to wake him. The disciples responded in a manner that the normal human being would do. They thought that Lazarus was taking a siesta, but Jesus was saying that Lazarus was dead.

Jesus informed them that He was going to see Lazarus. As Jesus was on His way some people saw Him and told Martha who encouraged Mary to go with her to see Jesus, but Mary refused and remained at home.

A soon as Martha saw Jesus, she began to speak to Him in a manner that seemed as though she was blaming Him for the death of her brother. Jesus explained to Martha that it was fine because her brother would live again. When Jesus reached Bethany He heard that Lazarus had been in the grave for four days so by then he was decomposed.

Martha retorted that she was aware of the fact that her brother would rise again in the resurrection when everyone would be resurrected. Jesus assured her that He was the Resurrection and the Life. In Him is life even if someone died. Jesus said that anyone who believes in Him has eternal life. He inquired of Martha of her belief in Him and what He had stated.

Martha then reported to Him that she believed that He was the Messiah, God's Son. She left and went to call Mary who came and fell at Jesus' feet, a form of worship. Mary reverberated the words that Martha spoke earlier, that if Jesus had been there, her brother would not have died. When Jesus observed her weeping and the people who were there weeping, He was moved with a hatred for death. He then asked them where they had interred him.

Jesus arrived at the grave and seeing the stone blocking the entrance, He instructed them to remove it. This command must have caused the crowd to wonder what in the world He was going to do. Martha again reminded the Master that by that time, a period of four days, he was now decomposed. Jesus had to repeat what He had stated earlier, that it was to give glory to God:

> [41b] Then Jesus looked up to heaven and said, "Father, thank you for hearing me.
>
> [42] You always hear me, but I said it out loud for the sake of all these people standing here, so they will believe you sent me."
>
> [43] Then Jesus shouted, "Lazarus, come out!"
>
> [44] And Lazarus came out, bound in graveclothes, his face wrapped in a headcloth. Jesus told them, "Unwrap him and let him go!" St John 11:41b-44 (NLT).

This miracle must have startled everyone standing there because a man who should have started to decompose was alive and well. Martha had a testimony; she would never doubt or question the Master again. I think that Lazarus thought that he was having a long nap, but when he glanced back from whence he came he knew that a miracle had taken place.

Calling From the Cross

Jesus and His Father had a good relationship, but when He came to earth and took on our sins His Father could not look at Him. At the end of His three year ministry He was placed on the Cross with the sins of the world. He felt abandoned by His Father, and He cried out in agony, [34b] "Eloi, Eloi, lema sabachthani?" which means, "My God, my God, why have you forsaken me?" Mark 15:34b (NLT)

Jesus cared about His mother, Mary, and although He had other siblings He felt responsible for His dear mother who stood in agony at the foot of the cross. Jesus was aware of the fact that His mother required someone very loving and compassionate to care for her, so He made the best preparation that He possibly could:

> [25] Standing near the cross were Jesus' mother, and his mother's sister, Mary (the wife of Clopas), and Mary Magdalene.
>
> [26] When Jesus saw his mother standing there beside the disciple he loved, he said to her, "Dear woman, here is your son."
>
> [27] And he said to this disciple, "Here is your mother." And from then on this disciple took her into his home. St. John 19:25-28 & 30 (NLT).

Jesus' call did not end here although it has taken a different form. Jesus had accomplished the mission that His father had sent Him to perform. He was thirsty, He, the Water of Life. He exclaimed, "I thirst!" John 20:28b (NKJV). The soldiers gave Him a piece of sponge that contained vinegar. Jesus received the sponge after which He cried out, "It is finished!" John 19:30a (NKJV).

When Jesus made the last pronouncement He was telling the Father that He had completed the work that He came to do on the earth. Jesus was faithful to the Father. He always spoke about pleasing His Father. He told everyone that He came to do His Father's will. He was an obedient man although He was total God yet He was total man. He had no other joy, but the joy to please Him that sent Him.

Saul

The Bible speaks of a renowned Christian assassin by the name of Saul of Tarsus who was not afraid to persecute the followers of Jesus. Saul had letters to enter homes, or synagogues and evict anyone he chose to take, whether male or female. This erudite man, who had one of the best teachers, was without mercy. He did not know Jesus, but he was defending God by eradicating the new sect, the followers of Jesus.

One day Saul and his choice men were heading to Damascus to attack the Christians and place them in chains to take back to Jerusalem, but a luminous light from heaven beamed down on him. The light was so bright that Saul was struck off his beast.

Saul suddenly heard his name called from heaven, [4b] "Saul! Saul! Why are you persecuting me?" Acts 9:4b (NLT). That was a strange voice for Saul, and the question did not sound logical. Saul did not see anyone, and surely he was not persecuting anyone who was brave enough to confront him. Saul had an encounter with the Lord Jesus. Saul was not satisfied so he asked Jesus who He was, and he did so respectfully. He received a reply instantaneously. [5b] "I am Jesus, the one you are persecuting! [6] "Now get up and go into the city, and you will be told what you are to do." Acts 9:5b-6 (NLT).

Sarah Young's Account

Sarah states in her Book "Jesus Calling," that her messages are meant to be read slowly, and in a place that is quiet. She encourages her readers to place their confidence in Jesus, regardless of the circumstances in their lives. Sarah states strongly, that in these troublesome times we are to be reminded of who God is. God has all the authority and Glory.

We are to think of how deep and broad God's love is, and no one can fathom His love. God is present and we have no need to fear when trouble tries to overwhelm us. God affords us the opportunity to grow in Him.

We are to adore God and praise Him. Sarah states that we cannot praise or thank God too much, because God dwells in the praises of His people. She wrote:

> [8] "I dwell equally in both types of praise. Thankfulness, also, is a royal road to draw near Me. A thankful heart has plenty of room for Me.
>
> When you thank Me for the many pleasures I provide, you affirm that I am God, from whom all blessings flow. When adversity strikes and you thank Me anyway, your trust in My sovereignty is a showpiece in invisible realms. Fill up the spare moments of your life with praise and thanksgiving. This joyous discipline will help you live in the intimacy of My Presence."

According to Sarah, Jesus explained that although He has all power both in heaven and earth, He is tender with us. She also states that the more we get feeble the more He is gentle to us. When we get weak, we should let it propel us into His presence, just as if we were entering an open door. Jesus knows that we will feel incomplete but we are reminded that He is there to assist us.

Jesus wants us to declare our trust in Him, just like we were placing coins in His bank; as we build up the stock of coins, when trouble comes we take from His treasury. Our Savior has promised that He will keep safe in His heart, all whose trust is invested in Him and He has even paid compound interest on our investment. When we invest in Jesus, during our quiet days, when all is peaceful, then when there is turmoil we will have more than enough to take us through. Sarah continued:

> [9] "I AM LEADING YOU ALONG THE HIGH ROAD, but there are descents as well as ascents. In the instance you see snow-covered peaks glistening in brilliant sunlight. Your longing to reach those peaks is good, but you must not take shortcuts. Your assignment is to follow Me, allowing Me to direct your path. Let the heights beckon you onward, but stay close to Me.
>
> Learn to trust Me when things go "wrong." Disruptions to your routine highlight your dependence on Me. Trusting acceptance of trials bring blessings that *far outweigh them all*. Walk hand in hand with Me through this day. I have lovingly planned every inch of the way. Trust does not falter when the path becomes rocky and steep. Breathe deep draughts of My Presence, and hold tightly to My hand. Together we can make it!"

Sarah states that Jesus encourages us to make an effort to trust Him fervently in all of the areas of our lives. We are to place our trust in Him in all circumstances of our existence. We are to cease wasting our strength, regretting how situations are, or how things will turn out, or even about what things might have been, just trust the Lord. Jesus wants us to begin taking things just as they are and look for His way, during those conditions.

Jesus reminds us that He is with us. We are human and there are changes in our life experience, but we are to remember that He is always present, protecting us. We may sometimes feel like we are having a free fall; people and things may let us down, but God is faithful and He is always with us. Jesus states that we are to depend on Him for assistance. He will hold our hand, and guide us all the way and then accept us into heaven.

Jesus calls on us to thank Him for sending the precious gift of the Holy Spirit. Her book imparts:

> [10] "This is like priming the pump of a well. As you bring Me the sacrifice of thanksgiving, regardless of your feelings, My Spirit is able to work more freely within you. This produces more thankfulness and more freedom, until you are overflowing with gratitude.
>
> I shower blessings on you daily, but sometimes you don't perceive them. When your mind is stuck on a negative focus, you see neither Me nor My gifts. In faith, thank Me for whatever is preoccupying your mind. This will clear the blockage so that you can find Me."

Jesus desires worship, and when we worship it should be done in "spirit and in truth." The angels and heavenly hosts are in the presence of God giving worship. There is constant worship taking place around the throne. Although we on earth cannot hear the heavenly hosts' unceasing worship, we are to resound praise and thanksgiving so that heaven will take notice.

We are certain that God in heaven hears our petitions, and requests, but it is our thankful shouts of praise that He requires. We can receive anything from His hands as long as He gets gratitude from us. The closer we get to Jesus, the more blessed we are. We receive His rich blessings, without limit. As we give praise and thanks to the Lord each day, we will receive Joy and Peace in His Presence.

CHAPTER SEVEN

THE SPIRITUAL CALL

The Repentance Call

Isaiah

I saiah called the people of Israel to repentance:

> 6 Seek the LORD while you can find him. Call on Him now while he is near.

> 7 Let the people turn from their wicked deeds. Let them banish from their minds the very thought of doing wrong! Let them turn to the LORD that he may have mercy on them. Yes, turn to our God, for he will abundantly pardon.

> 8 "My thoughts are completely different from yours," says the LORD. "And my ways are far beyond anything you could imagine.

> 9 For just as the heavens are higher than the earth, so are my ways higher than your ways and my thoughts higher than your thoughts.

> 10 "The rain and snow come down from the heavens and stay on the ground to water the earth. They cause the grain to grow, producing seed for the farmer and bread for the hungry.

¹¹ It is the same with my word. I send it out, and it always produces fruit. It will accomplish all I want it to, and it will prosper everywhere I send it.

¹² You will live in joy and peace. The mountains and hills will burst into song, and the trees of the field will clap their hands!

¹³ Where once there were thorns, cypress trees will grow. Where briers grew, myrtles will sprout up. This miracle will bring great honor to the LORD's name; it will be an everlasting sign of his power and love. Isaiah 55:6-13 (NLT).

Isaiah was one of the Major Prophets, one who encountered the Lord in a dynamic way. His was one of the first writing of the Biblical prophets. He was a very important scribe during the reign of the kings and after the death of King Uzziah his life changed. Isaiah saw the Lord for himself, because he was no longer working under Uzziah's shadow.

Jeremiah

Jeremiah, also a major prophet, was sent to Judah to state God's "case" to them. Although Jeremiah's message was different from Isaiah's, in that God was reminding Judah of the past, he still intended that his message would foster a change in the nation:

¹ Moreover the word of the LORD came to me, saying,

²Go and cry in the ears of Jerusalem, saying, Thus saith the LORD; I remember thee, the kindness of thy youth, the love of thine espousals, when thou wentest after me in the wilderness, in a land *that was* not sown.

³Israel *was* holiness unto the LORD, and the firstfruits of his increase: all that devour him shall offend; evil shall come upon them, saith the LORD.

⁴Hear ye the word of the LORD, O house of Jacob, and all the families of the house of Israel:

⁵Thus saith the LORD, What iniquity have your fathers found in me, that they are gone far from me, and have walked after vanity, and are become vain?

⁶Neither said they, Where is the LORD that brought us up out of the land of Egypt, that led us through the wilderness, through a land of deserts and of pits, through a land of drought, and of the shadow of death,

through a land that no man passed through, and where no man dwelt?

⁷And I brought you into a plentiful country, to eat the fruit thereof and the goodness thereof; but when ye entered, ye defiled my land, and made mine heritage an abomination.

⁸The priests said not, Where is the LORD? and they that handle the law knew me not: the pastors also transgressed against me, and the prophets prophesied by Baal, and walked after *things* that do not profit." Jeremiah 2:1-8(KJV)

God had an eternal love for His people and did not want them to continue in sin. He reminded them of what He had done for them, how He made provision for them, and He took care of them. God's people stiffened their necks and hardened their hearts, although they heard the voice of their God.

⁶ "The LORD said also unto me in the days of Josiah the king, Hast thou seen that which backsliding Israel hath done? she is gone up upon every high mountain and under every green tree, and there hath played the harlot.

⁷And I said after she had done all these *things*, Turn thou unto me. But she returned not. And her treacherous sister Judah saw it."

¹² "Go and proclaim these words toward the north, and say, Return, thou backsliding Israel, saith the LORD; and I will not cause mine anger to fall upon you: for I *am*

merciful, saith the LORD, *and* I will not keep *anger* for ever.

¹³Only acknowledge thine iniquity, that thou hast transgressed against the LORD thy God, and hast scattered thy ways to the strangers under every green tree, and ye have not obeyed my voice, saith the LORD.

¹⁴Turn, O backsliding children, saith the LORD; for I am married unto you: and I will take you one of a city, and two of a family, and I will bring you to Zion:

¹⁵And I will give you pastors according to mine heart, which shall feed you with knowledge and understanding." Jeremiah 3:6-7, 12-15 (KJV)

God continues to call the 'love of His life,' Israel, the one who walked away from a good Husband. He pleads with His people. He extends patience and everlasting love. God pleads with His people to return to Him as a good husband would to an unfaithful wife.

Hosea

God is sovereign and He uses wonderful illustrations to teach His children or to warn them. Hosea a minor prophet was instructed to go and marry a prostitute. Some of the children she gave birth to were from men with whom she had had relationships and the others were fathered by Hosea.

It is strange to hear God telling His prophet to marry a 'woman of the night,' instead of a virgin. We would look at a prostitute and say the worst things about her. No mother would appreciate her son bringing home a prostitute, informing her that here is my wife. That son would be considered out of his mind. God was using this illustration to show Israel their adulterous state:

> [15] "Then I will return to my place until they admit their guilt and look to me for help. For as soon as trouble comes, they will search for me."

> [1] "Come, let us return to the LORD! He has torn us in pieces; now he will heal us. He has injured us; now he will bandage our wounds.

> [2] In just a short time, he will restore us so we can live in his presence.

> [4] "O Israel and Judah, what should I do with you?" asks the LORD. "For your love vanishes like the morning mist and disappears like dew in the sunlight.

> [5] I sent my prophets to cut you to pieces. I have slaughtered you with my words, threatening you with death. My judgment will strike you as surely as day follows night.

^{6} I want you to be merciful; I don't want your sacrifices. I want you to know God; that's more important than burnt offerings.

^{7} "But like Adam, you broke my covenant and rebelled against me.

^{8} Gilead is a city of sinners, tracked with footprints of blood.

^{9}Its citizens are bands of robbers, lying in ambush for their victims. Gangs of priests murder travelers along the road to Shechem and practice every kind of sin.

^{10} Yes, I have seen a horrible thing in Israel: My people have defiled themselves by chasing after other gods!

^{11} "O Judah, a harvest of punishment is also waiting for you, though I wanted so much to restore the fortunes of my people!

^{1} "I wanted to heal Israel, but its sins were far too great. Samaria is filled with liars, thieves, and bandits!

^{2} Its people don't realize I am watching them. Their sinful deeds are all around them; I see them all!" Hosea 5:15; 6:1-2, 4-11; 7:1-2 (NLT)

God yearns for His people to repent. He loves His children and wants the best for them. They are unlike the other nations. Israel and Judah liked to play childish games, such as "In and out the window."

Amos

⁴ For thus says the Lord to the house of Israel:
"Seek Me and live;

⁵ But do not seek Bethel,
Nor enter Gilgal,
Nor pass over to Beersheba;
For Gilgal shall surely go into captivity,
And Bethel shall come to nothing.

⁶ Seek the Lord and live,
Lest He break out like fire in the house of
Joseph,
And devour it,
With no one to quench it in Bethel—

⁷ You who turn justice to wormwood,
And lay righteousness to rest in the earth!"

¹² For I know your manifold transgressions
And your mighty sins:
Afflicting the just and taking bribes; Diverting
the poor from justice at the gate.

¹³ Therefore the prudent keep silent at that time,
For it is an evil time.

¹⁴ Seek good and not evil, That you may live;
So the Lord God of hosts will be with you,
As you have spoken.

¹⁵ Hate evil, love good;
Establish justice in the gate.
It may be that the Lord God of hosts

Will be gracious to the remnant of Joseph.
Amos 5:4-7, 12-15 (NKJV).

God reminded erring Israel of their faults. He did not tell them for them to feel guilty, He informed them because He desired a change. A change from evil to good. God yearned for the fellowship that He had with His people. He is like a spouse who is spurned, but His heart still yearns for his spouse. God has given His people every reason to forsake evil and return to Him.

Israel was very ungrateful. God's people only ran to Him when they were held by the enemy with no way of escaping. When they were oppressed with no other nation or person to deliver them, then they accepted the call to repentance.

Zephaniah

God sent His prophet Zephaniah to ask His people to return to Him. He gave them the instruction as to how He wanted them to respond. He gave them time to repent. The Lord does not take people in ignorance or by surprise, He always gives a warning. God continues to be merciful:

> [1] "Gather together and pray, you shameless nation.
>
> [2] Gather while there is still time, before judgment begins and your opportunity is blown away like chaff. Act now, before the fierce fury of the LORD falls and the terrible day of the LORD's anger begins.
>
> [3] Beg the LORD to save you—all you who are humble, all you who uphold justice. Walk humbly and do what is right. Perhaps even yet the LORD will protect you from his anger on that day of destruction. Zephaniah 2:1-3 (NLT)

John The Baptist

Zechariah, a Jewish priest, resided with his wife Elizabeth, during the time when Herod was king of Judea. This couple was very old, and had no children. Elizabeth was barren, and must have been the talk of the town, when the other ladies, who were mothers, saw her; they would frown at her. Elizabeth was not popular, just because she was barren, and at this time, she had another strike to her name; she was old.

It so happened that Zechariah was serving in the temple, and he had a special visitation from an angel of the Lord. Zechariah was overcome with fear, but the angel calmed him down. The angel informed him that God had heard his prayers, and that his wife Elizabeth would have a son. If Zechariah had any doubt it should have dissolved because he also received the name of the baby, "John." John, would bring joy and happiness to his parents. God would make him great. John should not indulge in wine nor hard liquor, because he would be filled with the Holy Spirit before his birth, and this would result in him persuading the Israelites to return to the Lord.

Zechariah sought for a sign that what he was hearing was really true. The angel identified himself as Gabriel, who stands in God's presence, and yes, Zechariah would receive a sign. He would be dumb until the birth of the baby. Elizabeth became pregnant to validate the angel's message. When she was six months pregnant, she was visited by her young cousin Mary, who came with the most wonderful message in the world; young Mary was pregnant with the Lord Jesus. Mary was a virgin, so both women were walking miracles.

As soon as Mary greeted her cousin Elizabeth, the baby leapt in the womb of Elizabeth, just as the angel had stated. Elizabeth's pregnancy spread abroad and her neighbors and friends visited her, and rejoiced with her. Elizabeth gave birth to John; when she announced his name, her friends and relatives did not approve of it. They inquired of Zechariah the baby's name, and since he could not speak, he asked for a writing tablet on which he wrote the name John. He then spoke.

John grew up, and strangely, he resided in the wilderness; his clothes were made from camel's hair, and his food was locusts and wild honey. John was by the river Jordan, and people from Jerusalem and Judea flocked the region to hear him:

> [3]And he came into all the country about Jordan, preaching the baptism of repentance for the remission of sins;

> [4]As it is written in the book of the words of Esaias the prophet, saying, The voice of one crying in the wilderness, Prepare ye the way of the Lord, make his paths straight.

> [5]Every valley shall be filled, and every mountain and hill shall be brought low; and the crooked shall be made straight, and the rough ways shall be made smooth;

> [6]And all flesh *shall* see the salvation of God.

> [7]Then said he to the multitude that came forth to be baptized of him, O generation of vipers, who hath warned you to flee from the wrath to come?

> [8] Bring forth therefore fruits worthy of repentance, and begin not to say within yourselves, We have Abraham to our father: for I say unto you, That God is able of these stones to raise up children unto Abraham.

> [9]And now also the axe is laid unto the root of the trees: every tree therefore which bringeth not forth good fruit is hewn down, and cast into the fire.

[10]And the people asked him, saying, What shall we do then?

[11]He answereth and saith unto them, He that hath two coats, let him impart to him that hath none; and he that hath meat, let him do likewise.

[12]Then came also publicans to be baptized, and said unto him, Master, what shall we do? St. Luke 3:3-12 (KJV).

Although John did not look physically attractive, his message was straight-forward. He did not give the people who heard him any option. They were to repent, and One was coming to save them if they repented or destroy them if they refused to repent. I do not know how many of us would go to John's church from the description of his appearance. We are so accustomed to our padded seats, and John had trees and bugs. The message that John carried caught the people like the hook of a fisherman trapping a fish.

Knowing God and Going Forward With Him

> [3] Let us know, let us press on to know the
> LORD; his going forth is sure as the dawn;
> he will come to us as the showers, as the
> spring rains that water the earth. Hosea 6:3
> (RSV).

According to the Webster Dictionary:

> [11] Knowing: "The act or process of learning or
> perceiving something.—a Sagacious; expressive
> of the possession of inside information or secret
> knowledge."

When we know God it is more than just talking; it is intimacy; as someone states: "in-to-me-see." Knowing God is more than just casual, "Hello God," but it is spending time in His presence. The Bible presents a vivid picture of Mary, sitting at Jesus' feet while her sister Martha was busy preparing a meal.

Jesus had these friends: Martha, Mary and Lazarus, who resided in Bethany. Jesus and His friends stopped by the home of Mary and her siblings, and like a considerate hostess, Martha was busy preparing a sumptuous meal for her guests.

Something was wrong, Mary was not assisting her, so she brought it to Jesus' attention, although He was aware of it. Martha placed the blame on Jesus as she tried to make her sister feel guilty for not assisting. She asked Jesus if He did not care, seeing that her sister was not assisting her. Jesus' answer was very unusual. He explained that what Mary was doing, was the most essential act that was required, sitting at His feet was better than food.

It was thoughtful for Martha to feed the body, but sitting and getting to know Jesus was better. Everything has its place, but being in fellowship with Jesus exceeds everything. It was fine for Martha to cook, but she should have left Mary to listen to Jesus. Mary was very wise, because Jesus had just a short time on earth, so she had to savor that time with Him.

The Evangelical Commentary states:

> [12] "The crux of Israel's downfall throughout the Book of Hosea centers on the "lack of knowledge" of God (v.6). In the Western world today, we tend to define knowledge as something comprehended by the mind.
>
> "Knowledge" in Hebrew thought, then, is an issue of orientation. It is no surprise that Hosea targets the lack of true knowledge as Israel's greatest depravity. Because they have ignored God's law, the people will not stand in the gap as priests. As a result, the next generation will be ignored—a metaphor for the coming Assyrian exile."

Hosea had to know God, because it is abnormal for a clean man of God to be joined to a prostitute/harlot. When God instructed Hosea to marry that woman, Hosea must have thought he was going out of his mind. He could not see a loving God sending him to be joined with a lady of poor reputation. Hosea obeyed God although it was not making sense.

The Commentary goes on to explain that sin is personal, and it touches God, because of the rebellious person's attitude when he or she breaks his or her contract with God. Israel sinned when she broke the covenant that God had made. He would retain His blessings from them. Israel took the agreement lightly, and defied the very God who had their future planned; they broke the covenant.

The priests, who should have called the people closer to God, sinned against God as well and their sins increased. The Lord stated that He would change their glory into humiliation. God's judgement would fall upon both priests and prophets for failing to lead the people of God in the right path. The Evangelical Sunday School Lesson Commentary pointed out:

> [13] "The problem is certainly not that more priests need to be ordained! Indeed, the number of priests has been steadily increasing in Israel (V.7 NIV). The problem is that they are flippant toward sin. They do not understand that Yahweh is a covenant—making God, and to break His covenant is to write destruction. Not only this, but they do not understand their unique role as leaders.
>
> Although they wear the mantle of leadership and authority, they commit the same sins as the people they mean to lead. Their condemnation is seen most of all, though, not in their leadership but in their hearts. The Hebrew word for 'heart' (v.8) is *nephesh*, and refers to the totality of a person.
>
> They have directed themselves wholly toward sin, refusing to live as set apart. Therefore, God will not set them apart from the people when He unleashes His judgement.
>
> The sacred rhythms of the spiritual leadership of the community have not sustained the nation. As a result, priests will be swept away as if they were peasants. They will receive no special treatment. They remain primarily responsible for the sin of the nation."

The people received their own judgement as well. As recorded in the Bible in the book of Hosea, God charged them for the sin of whoredom. They had left Him for strange gods. God used Hosea as an example to illustrate His point to Israel. Hosea felt pain, but God still extended His unfailing love towards the ones who spurned Him.

After Hosea's harsh warning to Israel, he returned with a future of hope. God is now their father once more. Hosea brought hope to the people. God is a God of mercy, and Israel was fully aware of that:

> [1] Come, and let us return to the LORD; For He has torn, but He will heal us; He has stricken, but He will bind us up.
>
> [2] After two days He will revive us; On the third day He will raise us up, That we may live in His sight.
>
> [3] Let us know, Let us pursue the knowledge of the LORD. His going forth is established as the morning; He shall come to us like the rain, like the latter *and* former rain to the earth. Hosea 6:1-3 (NKJV)

Hosea was not pointing Israel to the temple at Jerusalem, although it was their worship center, he was pointing them to Jehovah or Yahweh instead. Again The Evangelical Sunday School Lesson Commentary pointed out:

> [14] "Hosea is certain that He is a God of redemption—He buys back what has been torn, smitten, and judged.
>
> Interestingly, Hosea does not downplay the reality of exile. He has already prophesied God's verdict on Israel's immediate future. They will be defeated, but this will be for a

preset amount of time, symbolized by two days in verse 2. Then, they will be revived from exile—a truth that all of the prophets agree on. And when they are revived from exile, they will be renewed as a nation. Their trajectory will change.

Even as the prophets struggle to accept the fact that during the exile it will look as if life for Israel is over, they continue to assert that exile will also be a time of purification for the people of God. God will return to His people to reestablish the covenant. Exile will be an opportunity."

Hosea knew God well enough, so his hope was in God's nature. Hosea knew what God felt when Israel turned their backs on Him, because Hosea was a jilted lover himself. Hosea had to take back his wife in the same manner in which God purchased Israel from the auction block. God knew that He could not totally depend on Israel. He was aware of the fact that very soon after the enemy was off their backs, they would be back to their former state, that is why he chastised them. Hosea was as a weapon in the hands of God used to bring judgement upon Israel. God wanted the people to have knowledge of who He was so He showed them mercy. The priests and the people offered sacrifice, but God's desire was that His people should know Him.

Hosea's prophecy introduces us to God as a Lover who extends His love to those who keep pushing away from Him. God desired that His people come back to Him although they never cease to be adulterous. Gomer was unfaithful to Hosea, and he continued to love her and in the same manner, God's people were unfaithful, but He continued to love them.

The book, A Call to Courageous Living, reminds us that we travel with the beginning of one step then another. It reminds the reader of men of faith who walked with God. These men Enoch, who walked with God;

Noah, who built an ark; Abraham, who left his homeland and loved ones to travel to an unknown destination, just because God said so; they knew God and placed their faith in Him and trusted Him regardless of the outcome. The above heroes of faith had courageous faith that caused them to trust God fully. Michael Catt wrote:

[15] "Long before he was a leader, Joshua had a record of obedient service and strong faith. Undaunted by the unbelief of his peers, Joshua was unwavering in his commitment. He was fearless in battle, and he was a godly man at home. Joshua was the total package, a man's man.

God's call to be courageous is undeniable. How we respond to that call determines our legacy.

The truly courageous man considers God in his calculations. He doesn't forget God in his daily life, only to search for Him in a crisis. He lives with a constant awareness that "I will be with you; I will not fail you or forsake you." Our strength comes from standing on the promises of Christ. At some point we move from calculation and contemplation to commitment.

Joshua was a great leader because he was a great follower. He understood duty and obedience. He knew there was an unseen hand guiding him and that God's judgment and analysis were better than his own reasoning. Many people are too big for God to use; they are too full of themselves.

Joshua's ability to conquer resulted from having been conquered by God.

Faithfulness in little things will open the door for bigger things. The landscape is littered with the lives of those who said they were going to do something great for God and failed to do it. We must renew our minds and think on these things because God has called us to think differently than the world thinks."

Michael further states that people who are fearful are often hesitant; he is making reference to Gideon who did not think he was valiant to go against the enemy, but because God's hands were on him he was able to accomplish his purposes. God is in search of a person whom He can trust with enormous responsibilities, and not someone who is gifted or who is a celebrity. God is looking for people who will ascribe unto him, glory. Gideon was fearful, having his eyes on the barriers, but he should have had courage, and looked forward to the opportunity that he had. Fear sees through fleshy eyes, while boldness always sees through eyes of faith. Michael continues:

[16] "Faith is fear that has said its prayers. The story of Ruth encourages us to be courageous. It should be a ray of hope in any difficult season.

The selfless response of Ruth to Naomi is the hinge on which the door of this story swings. What might seem on the surface like two insignificant women and one insignificant decision became one of the most pivotal moments of redemption history.

When life slaps you with the unexpected, you can choose to respond like Naomi or Ruth.

Naomi felt God had treated her unfairly, and she pointed at Him with an accusatory finger. Although no blessings had been promised that she could cling to, Ruth refused to spend the rest of her life wallowing in grief and self-pity. Rather, she put feet to her prayers and works to her faith.

Faith demands courage. It takes risks and acts according to God's Word. We can face an uncertain future or great loss or unexpected tragedy and grief with courage, knowing our heavenly Father cares for us and brings life out of death."

The author states that God is searching for men and women who are totally surrendered to Him. God listens for a response from those whom He calls, and the answer is either yes I will follow You or no I will not obey You. Some people say yes but the fact is, they have their own agenda; they know what they are looking for to gratify themselves and not God.

Elijah was an example of a man who prayed, and when he faced predicament, he trusted God for the answer. This prophet prayed on Mount Carmel before the fire fell. He knew that it was not because he was correct; but it was because of the God of Israel whom he was exalting why he was successful. When we face our "giants" we need to pray to God. We have to pray for our families; and after we have prayed, we must take courage in the Lord.

Nehemiah had to face criticism but he did so through prayer. He never allowed the enemies to have the upper hand. Whatever Nehemiah did was done through prayer. He knew that Jerusalem needed walls to protect those who were within, and to keep out the undesirables so he decided to build the walls, and although the enemies lied on him and tried in every way to dissuade him, he built the walls. Those who opposed him stated that "it could not be done, it should not be done, and it would not be done;" but through prayer and determination, it was done.

People who do not walk with God will be angered by you if you walk with Him. Our response to criticism will determine whether we are courageous or subdued. When Nehemiah was confronted by those who opposed him, he defeated them by praying and working on the project that he had started.

Nehemiah was succeeding, but the more progress he made, the more they assaulted him. Because Nehemiah was a reliable leader, he had the ability to continue to work, and that disturbed the troublemakers. These opposers of good work, seemed to have supporters on their side, and they even wrote letters to the authorities about Nehemiah, but God thwarted their attacks. Nehemiah's courage baffled his critics, which proved that if someone does not agree with the good job we are doing, we should never let them dissuade us.

Paul was an outstanding leader who could have chosen someone who was intellectual and brilliant, but instead, he chose a young man, by the name of Timothy. He was Timothy's mentor. Paul gave a pertinent piece of advice to Timothy that all of us especially young Christians need. Michael Catt puts it this way:

> [17] "The apostle reminded him to stir up the gift of God within him and not let the world intimidate him. The old apostle knew the fires of the early days of the church could go out if the next generation did not take seriously what had been entrusted to them.
>
> Many of us have bailed out on God over less significant things than what Timothy faced. We allow the fear of man to extinguish our fires. We worry about what others think or how they will talk about us at the coffee shop.

We worry about success and job security and follow the path of compromise.

It's time to stir up the gift, to jump into the arena. It's time to demand a higher calling than playing games. The sides aren't balanced; we are outnumbered. We must call people to the fire. The coals have been cold for so long that it takes time to stoke them and fan the flame again.

What will happen if we don't call out this generation to stir up the fire and sell out to the Savior? What could happen if we took seriously the command to "keep ablaze the gift of God" and to invest in a Timothy.

Many of us may never experience harsh persecution, but if we strive to delight in the Lord, and glorify Him, we will face persecution. Stephen was a man, "full of faith and of the Holy Ghost" who did not cower under severe persecution. He was probably a new Christian, but when the religious leaders interrogated him he was fearless. He used his trial platform to preach the good news about Jesus. The religious leaders did not want to hear about Jesus because they were the ones who sentenced Him to death; his testimony made them mad.

Stephen was wise, the Holy Spirit guided him, and he was able to stand firm and face his foes. He knew the scriptures and used them at the correct time, to witness for Jesus. As believers, we need to believe what we know and use it to win others to Jesus. Sometimes Christians are illiterate concerning the Scripture, so they do not have enough to defend them in times of trials. God wants us to be bold soldiers for Him.

Responding to God

Jesus told us of the cost of following Him:

> [24] Then Jesus said to the disciples, "If any of you wants to be my follower, you must put aside your selfish ambition, shoulder your cross, and follow me.
>
> [25] If you try to keep your life for yourself, you will lose it. But if you give up your life for me, you will find true life.
>
> [26] And how do you benefit if you gain the whole world but lose your own soul in the process? Is anything worth more than your soul? Matthew 16:24-26 (NLT).

Kay Arthur states that Jesus instructed us to count the cost. We have been asked to pay the price by denying ourselves, although this is not popular in our present-day Christian group. She explains:

> [18.] "The cost is death to self, when in our times many people are trying to discover self and take care of self. The cost is to follow Jesus as a habit of life for the rest of your life! That's not easy when you are playing it out in the world's court, and the grandstands are filled with a multitude shouting "Fool! You're a fool! Get off the court!"
>
> Oh, my friend, if you are going to deny yourself, take up your cross, and follow Jesus, you had better know with certainty whom you are following, what He is like, what He believes, how He lived in this adverse world,

and why and how He died. You also better
"know that you know" whether His death
was the end of it all or only the beginning."

God used John the Baptist to point the people to Jesus, and not to himself. In his "repentance message," John told the people what Jesus would do if they did not turn to Him. John had a ministry to fulfill and although it cost him his life in the end, he did what he was commissioned to do. The crowd went forward to be baptized by John. Like John, we are to follow Jesus. We are not to make excuses, and that is easy to do. We may talk of lack of training, or inadequacies, incompetency, or lack of experience, but that does not eliminate us from going forward and winning others to God. We are reminded that God did not call the wise, according to the flesh, neither did He call the strong, nor the eloquent, but He chose the lowly, as the world would call us, to expose those who see themselves as wise, and powerful.

God calls us and we do not chose where we want to go, or to do what we desire, He gives the command and we respond as a soldier does. We must show loyalty to Jesus first. We owe it all to Jesus and not to others whom we cherish. When Jesus calls us to follow Him, we must be reminded that He expects us to respond now and not at a later date. We must look ahead and leave the past life behind us, knowing of a surety that what is behind us, can never be equated to what He has in store for us.

Just like Mary, Lazarus' sister, we are encouraged to recline at Jesus' feet to be educated by Him. We are to learn of Jesus throughout our entire Christian life, and as Jesus told Martha, Mary had chosen the better part. We will be taught everything that will help us to learn what we must be, and that will assist us to do what we are supposed to. Our very prayer that we pray has its foundation in our relationship with our Lord, because we know who He is, His promise, and how we are to live. We must continue in persistent prayer.

Kay Arthur talks about us walking by faith instead of sight, although we find it easier to place confidence in the things that we can see. We are accustomed to trust in people and even ourselves than to place our trust in God to provide for us. We sometimes want to find out if God will make it happen for us. God knows what we need and if we place our trust in Him and seek His kingdom He will provide for our needs. Matthew Chapter Six tells us that He will take care of everything if we place Him first. We must believe in God no matter what circumstances we are experiencing. In her book, The Call to Follow Jesus, Kay explains the following:

[19] "It all boils down to a matter of faith, doesn't it? Whom will we trust, whom will we believe?

Thus says the LORD, "Cursed is the man who trusts in mankind and makes flesh his strength, and whose heart turns away from the LORD. For he will be like a bush in the desert and will not see when prosperity comes, but will live in stony wastes in the wilderness, a land of salt without inhabitant.

"Blessed is the man who trusts in the Lord. For he will be like a tree planted by the water, that extends its roots by a stream and will not fear when the heat comes; but its leaves will be green, and it will not be anxious in a year of drought, nor cease to yield fruit." (Jeremiah 17:5-8)

And without faith it is impossible to please Him, for he who comes to God must believe that He is and that He is a rewarder of those who seek Him. (Hebrews 11:6)."

The Bible informs us that God is aware of what is in our hearts; we can pretend to be different from who we really are to others, but not to God. We may "fool some of the people some of the times" but we cannot deceive God. He knows us more than we know ourselves. We may seem to elude God's wrath now, but one day, some day, we will have to give an account of the deeds that we have done in our bodies. We sometimes turn off the lights, and perform some of our actions in the darkness, but God sees through the darkest of night and He has the story from the conception to the end.

Some people promote evil deeds. They have others who condone with them in doing wrong, but God hates sin; all sin. We therefore have to walk right in the eyes of God. We have to live by the dictates of God's Word; our values and priorities have to be in proper order. We have to see beyond the things that are fleeting to those things that are eternal. We have to maintain a mindset to enter God's kingdom through the small and narrow gate, and let His Word guide and keep us. Kay Arthur continues:

[20.] "Faith and obedience seem to be synonymous when it comes to the kingdom of God. If we truly believe, then we do the things which God commands. And when we do what He has commanded, we ought to say, "We are unworthy slaves; we have done only that which we ought to have done" (Luke 17:10). Faith ought to obey. True faith is seen in its works; that is why Jesus said to the leper who returned to thank Him, "Your faith has made you well."

May we not get puffed up by all we do for the Kingdom of God. May we not trust in ourselves that we are righteous while viewing others as sinners. Instead, may we give thanks to the One who has been merciful to us as sinners (18:13).

As we wait for the day of the Son of Man, may we pray at all times and not lose heart, remembering that "there is no one who has left house or wife or brothers or parents or children, for the sake of the kingdom of God, who will not receive many times as much at this time and in the age to come, eternal life" (18:29,30).

We have to live according to the Word of God. Just to know the Word and become acquainted with it is not enough, we have to live it. We cannot be hypocrites in the church, we must have fellowship with the Word and with God. Jesus wept over Jerusalem, we do not want Him to weep over us, the church, His bride.

Called To Worship

In the book authored by Twila Paris and Robert Webber, Twila explains worship, which is her personal pledge:

> [21.] "Worship is the central focus of my life, and I want to tell you about my childhood so you can understand how worship became significant to me.
>
> I grew up as a preacher's kid, traveling in an itinerant ministry with my parents. I have been singing for as long as I can remember. My parents tell me that at age two and three I was already making up songs and singing them."

She wrote the song, "Come Worship the Lord," as an invitation to worship. The song strengthens us to reply to God because of His love. The center of worship is really about responding to a God who sustains us. God has delivered us from the power of evil, through Jesus our Lord, and because of that we have chosen to be obedient to His will. It does not matter the trials we are going through or the good times we are having, God's loving kindness and goodness still keep us. He has us in His hands, steadying us. It is enough reason to give God thanks. Twila also states:

> [22.] "I not only love to worship, I love to watch people who are worshipping. The psalmist says, "It is fitting for the upright to praise him" (Ps. 33:1). I read that verse one day, and as I meditated on it, it struck me with its truth. Sometimes when I'm in a group of people who are worshipping, particularly if they are singing with their eyes closed and their hands raised, I'll take a peek at them.

And I'm always impressed by how beautiful they look. People seem to glow and radiate when they worship.

I remember my grandmother used to say to me, "Oh Twila, blue is so becoming on you." She meant that I look good in blue. This idea also pertains to worship. Praise is becoming to the upright. When we worship, praise produces a radiant beauty on our faces because of our contact with God.

More important, in worship we are especially beautiful to God. Worship is a sweet aroma to God. For me, the fact that God loves our worship is a very challenging and motivating truth, a truth that I stress in all my worship songs. In my song, "This Celebration," I have tried to capture how our worship is pleasing to God. The song names who God is and praises for God's person. Of course, this is what we do when we gather together to worship: we lift up our hearts in response to God."

Robert Webber comments that he sees many people who go to worship in a thoughtless attitude, without thinking about what they are about to do. They present themselves where worship is taking place with little or no idea of what worship is about. He was also guilty of the same, until one Sunday when his pastor proclaimed that he was going to teach some classes on worship. Although Webber thought that that subject would be appropriate, and interesting, he could not recall anything that was said on that topic. He thought that the topic was either not thoughtful or challenging. He decided to investigate the topic for himself.

He began by finding fault with worship. As he pondered about the topic, he concluded that a lot of the worship was too intellectual. Webber began to visit other churches to satisfy his longing soul. Some of the churches were the reverse of his church because they were filled with emotion. He concluded that the service was not worship but evangelism instead. He also thought that worship must be different from evangelism. After examining various forms of worship, he was dissatisfied, so he consulted the Scripture, to find out what the Word says about worship. The entire Bible from Genesis to Revelation is about Christian worship. The Bible has many expressions of worship; the books of Psalms and Revelation are examples of heavenly hymns. The Old Testament speaks of the worship of the Tabernacle and the Temple. The New Testament talks of worship in singing, baptism, preaching, and communion. Webber wrote:

[23] "I was visiting an evangelical church in the Wheaton area where I live, and the associate pastor prayed a prayer that I will never forget. After an opening hymn he said, "Let us pray," and these are the words that came out of his mouth:

"Lord, we bless You for creating us in Your image. And we thank You that after we fell away from You in sin, You did not leave us in our sin, but You came to us in Jesus Christ who lived among us, died for us, was buried and rose again, and ascended into heaven. And now, O Lord, as we await His coming again, receive our worship in His name."

When he prayed those words I said, "that's it, that's it." I wanted to leap on the pew in front of me and do a dance because he struck right at the heart of what we do in worship.

When we gather to worship, we proclaim, enact, remember, and celebrate the story of

God's redeeming love. Twila captures this theme in her song "Come Worship the Lord" when she connects our worship with God's loving-kindness and mercy. If it had not been for God's loving-kindness and mercy there would be no story to tell, to remember, to celebrate. But God did not leave us in our sins. God rescued us, and worship celebrates the rescue, the saving event."

Worship is not about us or the experience that we have, it is about God, about the One who saves us. When we think of Him saving our souls from hell, we will begin to worship; that is sufficient to make us worship. When we worship, God does what He usually does from the beginning, He reaches out to us, and delivers us from the pain and pressures of sin. He invites us to come from the things that bother us to His throne of grace, and makes a contract with us. He brings us into a relationship with Himself that brings us healing and steers us toward the Promised Land, just as He brought the children of Israel through the Red Sea into the land flowing with milk and honey. We then respond with heartfelt praise and gratitude towards our God. We lift Him up and worship Him for all that He has done. When we remember how He saves us, we will worship because that is what He desires of us.

My pastor caught the vision to reiterate to us his teaching regarding the importance of worship. He instructs us to "bow down and worship God." He leads us into worship before he preaches. He cries, he glorifies God for who He is. Many in our congregation fall on their knees, and give honor to our God. The faces of the worshippers express heartfelt gratitude to our wonderful Lord, because some of us know the story of where He brought us from. The worship continues in my church.

When we worship we are enacting the story that gives meaning to the church's existence in this world. We have to be faithful to the biblical form of worship. God desires His people to model the death and resurrection which we recall in worship, to make us into special individuals. He desires us to die continually to sin's power, and be resurrected in the Spirit. When we worship we do not only remember how God saved us, but how He shapes us by His deeds into the people of Christ.

Webber begins to address our "Broken Relationship With God." He alludes to Adam and Eve, our first parents, how they disobeyed God. Their sin came down into our bloodline, and so we are guilty of envy, murder, strife, deceit and malice. We are guilty of a "Broken Inner Self." We war inside. Cain in the Bible warred with himself and slew his own brother. Although God made us for Himself, we make gods of ourselves or some other created being or thing.

We have "A Broken Relationship With Our Neighbor." We are guilty of having fights with others. There have been broken relationships all over the world. There has been fighting and wars for many, many years. He speaks of the "Broken Relationship With Nature." Although the Lord created the world and all that is in it for His glory, we observe nature misbehaving itself. There is pollution in the air and in the water. We are told of the change in the ozone layer, places that were cold are experiencing warmer conditions while places that were hot are noticing colder conditions. We hear of the melting of the ice in certain areas so the animals that reside there are in danger. Man was made to serve God, but man believed the lies that Satan told so Satan is running all over the earth, and man is serving him instead of God. Webber continues:

[24] "As I began to understand this four-fold extent of sin, I began to realize how utterly impossible it is for me, a participant in this sinful condition, to approach God in worship. Here is the scenario: because we have turned from God, distorted ourselves, set off a chain of cosmic broken relationships, and damaged the nature of social relationships, we have created a society full of conflict. Our rebellion against God has resulted

in a culture in which relationships within marriage, the family, work, and all of society are in disarray.

The whole world is in a bad situation, a state of sin. And no one is exempt. Each of us participates in the human condition of sinfulness. And in this condition we cannot worship God."

We have a challenge to recognize that when we come to worship, we come out of our sins and our broken relationships with God, our self, our neighbor and nature. We have to remember that we rebelled against God and have offended Him in so many ways.

Our sins have prevented us from going to God in worship on our own volition. Jesus is our Mediator, so we come to the Father through Him, and He heals our relationships. When we come to God, we come through the blood of Jesus, His only Son whom He gave to pay for the sins of the world. We come to God knowing that we have sinned, but we experience salvation through the blood of Jesus Christ, so we have a right to give God thanks and praise, only because of Jesus. The world cannot worship God and they do not want to worship Him. The world cannot speak for itself because it does not want to repent, so the church speaks for the world.

When we gather to worship, we are bringing the sins of the entire world, and all their broken relationships, to our God. Our worship is offering to the Father, the work of Jesus. Only He can mend the broken relationship with God, and bring restoration. We worship by giving thanks in Jesus' name.

We worship in the sanctuary, and the smallest sanctuary is our heart where we commune with God alone. We communicate: talk to God and He talks to us. The larger sanctuary is where we congregate, whether in a home or in a church. We call it our meeting place, this is where worship takes place. When we worship alone, we do not have to worry about our language or the content of our conversation, we have a time with God all by ourselves. We sometimes choose what to say when we gather collectively; it sometimes sound polished or in other words rehearsed material for the listening ears. God is so wonderful that He can touch our hearts during worship, and take us out of self and cause His spirit to flow through us.

When Twila worships through songs, she realizes that she is not singing alone, but the whole of God's people, the redeemed, are responding to God. Corporate worship is very special, it is like going to the grandparents' home for Christmas and the entire family is enjoying the sumptuous meal. As we gather together in God's house to worship, we have a longing to be together again, and again. God's name, His throne, God's love are all proclaimed from our hearts, thoughts and mouths.

Baptism is discovered to be the antidote that brings healing to the relationship with God. This has been a part of worship from the inception of the church. When the author was baptized she renounced the work of Satan as she was immersed in the name of the Father, Son and Holy Spirit; many of us had the same baptism. The early church had a different custom, the person who was being baptized, spat in the direction of Satan and broke his or her tie with sin. Twila states:

> [25] "When Jesus commanded His disciples to, "'Therefore go and make disciples of all nations, baptizing them in the name of the Father and of the Son and of the Holy Spirit'" (Matt. 28:19), He had in mind that indissoluble union between Himself and the church that is expressed in a restored relationship. This is borne out by His concluding statement: "'And surely I am with you always to the very end of the age'" (Matt. 28:20). God's presence is both personal and corporate in the church. The life of the believer is lived out in the context of the church, Christ's body. Thus, the statement of

the church father, Cyprian (A.D. 250), that "he who has not the church for his mother has not God for his Father" stands. Baptism symbolizes our entrance into the church, the community of God's restored people.

Next, I discovered that the broken relationship which I experienced in my inner self and the loss of self-worth which came from that ruptured inner self found a place of healing in the church and in its worship.

Self-worth is derived not from anything we have done but from the realization that we are remade in the image of God. Paul spoke of the Christian as "to be made new in the attitude of your minds; and to put on the new self, created to be like God in true righteousness and holiness" (Eph. 4:23-24). Having been remade in the image of God, we receive a restored sense of our task and function in the world. No one is without value or not important to the body. Everyone has something to contribute. This means of course, that in the church, we need to help each person find his or her unique gift and exercise it to the benefit of all. When the gifts God has given to us are accepted and used in the church, our own sense of self-worth is intensified."

Worship is the true expression of the church, God's children on this planet, earth. The church is worship, and not just something that it does. Worship discloses the very character of the church, because it is the ultimate goal of human's history; man was born to give worship to God. When the church worships, it is really the presence of what is to come. In the new heavens and new earth there will be worship, so the church is in a rehearsal stage for the grand finale. When we worship, heaven comes down to us, and pulls us into an experience of restored relationship with God, with ourselves, with our neighbor and with nature. As we worship, we experience a taste of the heaven that is to come. Webber concludes this chapter in the book with the following:

[26.] "Allow me to close this chapter with an example of the future orientation of worship. It comes from African American worship. As you know, deep in black genetic history is a sense of dislocation with the culture of this world. On the plantation blacks were "niggers," a term that meant they were nobody. They could be sold on the block like cattle, children could be sent off never to be seen again, and the plantation owner could do whatever he pleased with their lives.

But when the blacks assembled to do church they entered a new world, the Promised Land. Here they were relocated with God and no one was "nigger." Everyone was "brother" and "sister," and the reality of a new world, a new order of things was experienced, even though it was ever so brief.

So, here is our challenge. Like our African American brothers and sisters, let's learn how to do church in our worship. Let's enter into that heavenly realm and worship with the angels, the archangels, and the entire heavenly host. For in worship we are momentarily united with heavenly worship and gather with the saints around the throne and do church. And in this momentary experience of the heaven which is to come, the church now is a prefiguring of the healing brought to all broken relationships—with God, self, neighbor, and nature—and an actual experience of this healing now in our earthly life."

Our worship is supposed to be a response to God; His character, what He has done, in restoring our lives, how He touches us, how He heals us, and for making us complete. The worship songs that we sing are in answer to His healing and saving presence. Worship songs link people with the heavenly throng, the angels, archangels, cherubim, and seraphim, who present their praises to God repeatedly. When people worship they are responding to God who is present through songs, prayers, sermons, communion and many other ways by which He shows up in our worship. When God is speaking and acting in our midst, we raise our hearts, our voices, our hands, and our entire self to respond to Him.

When we worship, whether in public or private, we do so in response to God who is and to God who acts. We never initiate worship; it is God who initiates worship, because He is the One who is always reaching out to us. We respond to God for reaching out to us.

The Scripture tells us how we are to be saved from the power of sin, and how to enter in the fullness of life. There are many religions in the world and they somehow talk about being saved from something or the other. The Christian religion is different, and is very unique in that it offers a way of escape from this world and it's evils. The religion of the Bible is a religion of this world and also of the one that is to come. Christianity gives hope that is different from myths and New Age false religion because it is religion for the present age and for the world to come.

God extends Himself to us in the person of Jesus Christ regardless of our situations in life and this rests in the heart of the Scripture story, and therefore, of our worship. God called Abraham and developed a relationship with him, and this relationship continued to his descendants, the patriarchs, to Israel, through His covenant at Mt. Sinai, with the prophets, and with Jesus. God, through the Holy Spirit searches us out. God is ever maintaining us, repairing the broken relationship, settling us, and strengthening our relationship with Him. Genuine worship is God extending Himself to us wherever we are, just as He did to the great men and women of the Bible, and we in turn reach back to Him in response.

We observe people in the Bible who reached out to God in worship just as we do. Zaccheaus climbed a tree to see Jesus, there was a ruler who came to Jesus by night, there was blind Bartimaeus, we also think of the woman who touched the hem of Jesus' garment, the demoniac, and yes the disciples who were being tossed by a storm on the sea. It is God who reaches out to us at first, and we respond. Webber continues by saying;

[27.] "An important feature of the Christian faith and of worship is that it never denies who we are. Because we are God's people made in God's image, God reaches out toward us in the fullness of who we are. For example, God is a God of imagination. Everything that is, God made out of nothing. God formed the world and gave it shape and color. Every blade of grass, every cloud formation, every insect, all the colors of the rainbow, and the intricacies of the human body and mind were all imagined and created by God. Because God is a God of imagination who made imaginative people, God reaches out to us through the use of our God-given imagination.

But what does all of this have to do with our worship? How do we respond to God in our imagination? I think it is important for us to recognize how our imagination is used in worship. Processions, baptisms, the

celebration of the Table of the Lord, the
great festivals of Christmas and Easter all
touch our imagination. That is, they are
visual, tactile, colorful, action-oriented acts
of worship that usually recall God's saving
events and literally bring us to the throne
of God to worship not only with our hearts,
our bodies, and our minds, but also with
our imaginations. In this way we return
God's gift of imagination to God in an act of
response, and that response is our worship."

When we worship, we are responding to God who saved us. He is a God
who speaks and acts, and our worship is always a response to Him who
reaches out to us. We are to worship purposefully. We are to resolve that
we will not conceal anything from the Lord, we are to approach Him
regardless of our condition. When God speaks to us we should answer
with a language of praise. We will also bow down and glorify His name
that is above every other name.

Christians are familiar with the topic of going to the mountain to
worship. The author has a view of people moving towards the mountain
where they would congregate in the presence of God. Isaiah made
reference of the people of God assembling at the mountain. Moses was
one who would go to the mountain to meet with God. The Scripture
generally speaks of worshipping in the mountain. Abraham told his
servants that he and the lad were going to worship. Jesus was sometimes
at the Mount of Olives; He was even transfigured on the mountain.
Webber also wrote:

28. "The biblical notion of assembling could
apply to any fellowship. In all churches
of the world the people are streaming in
and then streaming out. We stream to the
fellowship of our church to worship; there in
that place, at that mountain of God, we are

built up, established equipped, encouraged, challenged. Then we are sent out to go and spread the Kingdom of God.

Picture this: we have streamed in from all parts of our city or town to assemble, and there in the gathering we bring an offering of praise and worship. Our song joins the great eternal song of the heavenlies as we gather around the throne with that great company of saints. We lift our voices together with them—crying, shouting, and singing, "To him who sits on the throne and to the Lamb be praise and honor and glory and power, forever and ever!" (Rev. 5:13).

I know that when I'm among the assembled people that God is here in our midst. The King is here seeking to rule in our hearts right now. So this concept that where two or three are gathered, there He is in our midst is a powerful truth. It challenges us because sometimes when we gather for worship, we simply go through the motions. I know I've done that a number of times, and others have told me they have done the same. But I remind myself and others that whenever the people of God gather in a theater, in an arena, or in a church for worship, God is there."

Twila makes an important observation, in stating that church begins as we begin our journey toward the sanctuary. She further states that worship begins when we assemble ourselves for church. Just by waking up, putting on our garments, getting into our transportation, and getting to church for worship is the first phase of worship. As we gather together for worship, we are told that we are not there to entertain the crowd but because God has called us to be "lights of the world," as well as "salt of the earth." We are then ready to tell of the story how God recovers us from a place of darkness, so we offer Him praise and thanksgiving for the wonderful work that He has done in our lives, by making us the people of God, and joint-heirs with Jesus Christ. When we enter the parking lot of our churches, the forces of evil should be terrified of us. We should be a picture of the overcomers who will be assembling once again to bind the powers of evil and derail the devil's intentions. We should be a picture of a people of the new kingdom, who love and serve each other.

We know that God is a Spirit, so when we worship we do so in the Spirit. God came down to earth in the person of His Son Jesus Christ, to be one of us, "earthly." Consider God in a natural world, suffering in the flesh, operating in the flesh to draw us to His Father; He became one of us so that we became like Him. The Holy Communion is a reminder to us of Jesus' death, burial and resurrection; it is also a physical side of our worship. As we partake of the communion we remember Jesus' victory over the forces of evil, and we celebrate the victory that was accomplished at the Cross, and in our lives through worship. It is wonderful to perceive that when we pray and give thanks over the elements of communion we are really celebrating all of God's saving work from time began, through to the time when Jesus saved us.

Worship has two folds: we give glory and honor to God, and God, through Jesus Christ subdues all the powers of evil through His death and resurrection for us. He has brought healing to all the people of the world. In worship, we receive a taste of His healing, as just a "down payment on our eternal treasure." It is vital for the church to provide time and opportunity in worship for those who need healing. This can be done through preaching, prayer, singing, communion, and the anointing with oil.

The Holy Spirit dwells in the church, especially in our worship. Our bodies are the temples of the Holy Spirit, so when we worship we grow in our Spirit. This spiritual growth helps us to commune with God the Father through Jesus, by the Holy Spirit. It is the business of the Holy

Spirit to make us grow. Although Jesus is the Mediator between God and man, it is the Holy Spirit who is the Messenger between God and the human race. It is the working of the Holy Spirit into our hearts that causes us to be changed into the image of Jesus. Webber informs us:

[29.] "Worship transfers events through recitation and rehearsal. The service of the Word, which consists of reading Scripture and preaching, is an oral recitation of those past events that continue to give meaning to our lives today. A good communicator in reading and preaching is one who can make the events of the past come alive. Preaching re-creates the event and brings it to us by the power of speech. The Holy Spirit works through that proclamation in such a way that the hearer experiences the original event and therefore responds to it in a way similar to those who were actual witnesses.

Participation in worship is not meant to be rote or casual. It requires an active I'm-really-there-with-Christ approach. It is something the church does, not something the church observes.

The meaning of what is happening is, of course, rooted in the actual historical event. But the experience of that meaningful event is now being re-created in the worship of the church. By going through worship in faith, the believer is using his or her mind, body, emotions, and senses to remember and to give thanks. At the same time his or her senses are opened to God's grace."

CHAPTER EIGHT

♈

UNDERSTANDING YOUR CALL

William and Catherine Booth

G ary McIntosh and Glen Martin speak about five ways to find people. They quoted Casey Stengel:

> [30] "It's easy to get good players. Gettin' em to play together, that's the hard part." What is true in baseball is also true in the ministry of the local church. At least five key players or strategies must be united and balanced in a local church to achieve effective evangelism."

The authors listed five outstanding persons, and groups who have an understanding of their call; Campus Crusade, and its leader, Dr. Bill Bright, Billy Graham, The Salvation Army, The Navigators and "production evangelism."

Bill Bright the founder of Campus Crusade for Christ, had a tremendous burden to declare Jesus on the college campus. He wanted young people to know Jesus and although his message was so profound, it was compelling. Bill was so humble that when he signed his letters he referred to himself as one who was fulfilling "The Great Commission" in this age, then he wrote "Bill."

Billy Graham is one of the greatest evangelists of our time, he reached the world by persuasion. His entire life has been spent telling the world about Jesus, who is mighty to save. He preached to millions of people world-wide and was able to convince people to respond to the gospel without twisting their arms. He is like the apostle Paul who knew Jesus, and so he persuaded all men to come to Him. He was an effective preacher and although he does not preach now, the legacy continues, his tapes continue to draw sinners.

The Navigators is a group that assists others to see the desire for discipleship or "progression evangelism." The Navigators group states;

> 31. "You can lead a soul to Christ in from 20 minutes to a couple of hours, but it takes from 20 weeks to couple of years to get him on the road to maturity, victorious over the sins and recurring problems that come along."

The Navigators have a yearning to see the Christians progress. They follow Jesus' words "make disciples" as their focus from the Word. They also have follow-up programs and literature that they use to disciple the disciples. The "production evangelism" educates church members on how to be witnesses for Jesus. This group instructs people on how to share their faith.

The Salvation Army is an organization that is aware of their call; they make themselves available in times of crisis. They are an extension of the hands of Jesus in countries all around the world. They take Jesus' words to heart when He said,

> 32. "For I was hungry, and you gave Me something to eat; I was thirsty, and you gave Me drink; I was a stranger, and you invited Me in; naked, and you clothed Me; I was sick, and you visited Me; I was in prison, and you came to Me" (Matt. 25:35-36).

The founders of The Salvation Army, William and Catherine Booth dedicated their lives to this cause. They were evangelists. Their work was very successful so they had an outstanding ministry. The Booths dedication to God's work caught the eyes of one Reverend Dr. William

Cooke, who had seen their tremendous potential, and encouraged them to be a part of the New Connexion work in London. Dr. Cooke informed them that the lives of Christians would be changed, and that they would be taught to honor Jesus, through their ministry.

William and Catherine accepted the offer and were doing tremendously well for the Lord. Their work was very influential and they began to have revival meetings all over England. The Reverend Dr. Cooke became jealous of their great success and launched an attack against the Booths. William was effective at his call for five years and during those years his critics, leaders of the church, were plotting against him. The first of these attacks took place when William held a series of meetings in Nottingham, and the superintendent started to oppose his work. All William was doing, was answering his call, because he "understood" his call.

In those days the circuit consisted of small churches, some of which were held in homes. They had very large groups as well which were too large for homes, so they required churches. The people in the circuit prayed together, studied together and worshipped together, so if one person opposed William, then everyone would follow suit. It would be difficult for William to continue to preach in that organization.

William seemed to take Christianity to a higher level than what those in the circuit were accustomed to, because their Christianity was based on being polite, and having private behavior. William had lists made of those who needed salvation, or those who required renewing their commitment. They were prayed for by their names being called out in public, prior to the beginning of the revival services. There was a problem; some of the names that were on the lists were the outstanding members of the local churches, civic leaders, and prominent business people. Their concern was that they were marked as "sinners" and that was very embarrassing, demeaning, and quite likely very slanderous.

When the meetings began those who were in attendance were given the opportunity to make a public commitment to Jesus Christ. They had to show their allegiance by stepping forward and kneeling in the presence of all those who were in attendance. Some of the leaders of the New Connexion disapproved of the way the meetings were conducted. They believed that the people were forced to make a decision to follow Jesus, so they would backslide later on.

The new converts and lay people were delegated to do important duties that were once done by the ordained ministers. Women were not allowed to minister in those days because some Christian leaders were following the command in the Bible where it states that women must remain silent in the church. Now that William was using them to minister, they were placed over men instead of being "submissive" to men. Catherine was also working in the ministry and that gave the leaders more evidence to move William out of his position. Catherine could not be stopped; she was an advocate for women especially in the area of worship, teaching, and leadership, in the church. She had been busy since she married William. In her book, William and Catherine Booth, Helen Hosier wrote:

> [33.] "Whatever the exact cause or Wright's opposition to William's preaching methods, it is clear that much of the problem was a simple matter of jealousy. William was such a dynamic speaker and drew such large crowds that he made most of the other pastors in the New Connexion look very inadequate by comparison.
>
> William and Catherine were committed to their approach to ministry, however, and served in several communities, including Gateshead, a town of fifty thousand, located just across the river Tyne from Newcastle, on the northeastern coast of England. By the summer of 1860, William had become quite ill. The combined pressures of pastoral

duties and evangelistic endeavors were partly to blame. The stubborn unwillingness of New Connexion leaders to assign him to full-time evangelism added more stress. The attacks on Catherine because of her work at Gateshead and her outspoken advocacy for women in the church also weighed heavily on him. It took months for William to recover his health. During that time, Catherine took over virtually all of his duties.

Soon, her remarkable abilities were clear to all, and her fame as "the woman preacher" was spreading far beyond Gateshead. But this was a time when most Victorian women wore gloves, carried delicate fans, and kept their pretty mouths shut, at least in public. Catherine's strong opinions and great success as a preacher combined with William's uniquely powerful ministry soon had many leaders in the New Connexion whispering, "These independent Booths need curbing."

In December 1860, William returned to his work at Gateshead, and on Christmas Day, he and Catherine shared the preaching duties at Bethesda Chapel.[2] During the first few months of 1861, Catherine began to regularly accept invitations to preach in public—and not just as a replacement for her ailing husband. The last restraints on her role in their shared ministry were cast aside.

Catherine had grown very frustrated with New Connexion Methodism and was urging her husband to consider an independent ministry of some kind. But she was also willing to stay at Gateshead, so long as "the Lord's leading" was their first priority. [4] She also had some anxious thoughts about the future. She was now the mother of four young children. They had a good home and a settled income, but only so long as they remained at Gateshead. The membership of Bethesda Chapel had grown dramatically and the Sunday services were crowded, but Catherine was concerned about her husband's health, as well as her own."

In 1861 William and Catherine were treated like animals by the Connexion. They were no longer wanted in that ministry and not because of any sins that they had committed. God was not finished with them because He had a door open that would last a whole life time.

Catherine gave herself to the work of the Lord. She prayed publicly in the first Sunday service, and that was as controversial as preaching for women in those days. She was involved in teaching class meetings and Bible study. Catherine started to visit homes in the more impoverished parts of the town and committed two evenings per week to this service. She felt sorry for the poor as she visited each and saw their suffering. She informed her husband of the condition of the women she visited. Since the Booths were banned from the Wesleyan pulpits, William began to go to simple places. Helen continues:

[34.] "Early the next year, William and Catherine began a series of meetings at Cardiff, in Wales. They were denied access to the main chapels in the area and so were forced to find new places to hold services. They rented a large, indoor arena and also used a circus tent. This was considered a radical departure at the time, but it created unique opportunities for them to reach people who did not feel comfortable in church buildings. When derelicts and prostitutes were converted, William's joy seemed particularly profound.

The Booths soon concluded that people who lived in a world of saloons and honky-tonks often found a tent flap more inviting than the heavy door of a stately church. They also discovered that these secular surroundings had advantages for the Christians who came to the services. Without the visible signs of denominational loyalty to remind them of their differences, many believers began to experience a sense of unity in Christ that had been almost unknown to them before.

Friendships were established at Cardiff that would be critical to the development of the Booths as individuals and to the success of their ministry for years to come. Wealthy ship owners John and Richard Cory were deeply moved by what they saw and heard at the services. They quickly offered to underwrite the expenses of the work. Later they would provide critical financial support during the early days of The Salvation Army, support that would continue for fifty years. Marian Billups would become a lifelong friend to Catherine, and both she and her husband would be important early supporters of The Salvation Army.

William and Catherine were not the only ones worried about the resistance that kept appearing to revivalism in England. Charles

Spurgeon, the well-known Baptist preacher, commented on it in an article published by the *Baptist Almanac in 1863*.

In "A Call to the People of God," he wrote: "The present state of our Churches fills me with alarm. The gracious revivals of the last few years were indications of the Lord's readiness to work in the midst of our land . . . I fear that we have slighted a golden opportunity which may not return while any of this generation are alive . . . Communities which despised the revival are confirmed in their sin by its manifest subsidence . . . ."[8]

In spite of all their success, this was a difficult time for William and Catherine."

As time went on, William and Catherine decided that they would be more effective, in multiplying their work for the Lord if they had separate campaigns, so Catherine started to conduct her own revival meetings. The Booths needed more funds, so they published and sold a hymnbook, along with pamphlets that were authored by Catherine. Catherine also received invitations to preach in another area of London. Hundreds of adults and children accepted the Lord as Catherine ministered to them. William and Catherine were accepting other invitations in areas of London, and northern England; their meetings were extremely successful.

Catherine ministered in the organization of: "The Midnight for Fallen Women." She informed William of the sickness and poverty of those people in that organization. It got so severe that seven-year-old girls had to work fourteen-hour days, with the whipping of their overseer's strap to keep their eyes open; poor women were in the brothels, and some of the children had cholera and smallpox. There was a group of children, ages four to sixteen who were placing sandpaper on matchboxes; one of the boys had a broken spine, so he knelt to do his work. An account was given of a mother who was dying while she watched her three children at work. A child who was almost four years old had to work five hours each day and another child had to work from 10:00 am to 9:00 pm.

The Booths created The East London Christian Revival Society, which was later renamed, The East London Christian Mission, and later The Christian Mission. Catherine was the counselor at the earlier stage of this organization. William was not paid for his services but God provided friends who gave them gifts, and Catherine received money when she spoke to wealthier people known as the "West Enders."

William was having a tremendous effect on the lives of people in the East End of London, near the London Hospital. His nightly meetings drew hundreds of working men and others to Jesus. The services that William, the devoted man of God, held were so successful that he acquired a large hall in the neighborhood for his evangelistic effort before the winter began. The Salvation Army was born out of his work, although the name Salvation Army was not given to the organization as yet. The purpose of the organization was in clear view.

Helen further states:

> [35.] "For the most part, simple people of limited ability responded to Booth's call for help. The giants of forceful leadership would come later. In those early days, William Booth stood quite alone at the head of the army that was in the making. He had hoped for an enlistment of a hundred who would stand with him; the actual number was only sixty. And after the first year, many of those left for one reason or another—some found his teaching on the truth of sanctification not in keeping with their own beliefs; still others considered that he laid too much stress

upon repentance and good works. His way of conducting prayer meetings gave offence to some, and others didn't like the penitent form. But it was mainly the mocking and mobbing by the crowds in the streets that was too much for the endurance of the less zealous. And, in all fairness, it should be acknowledged that some left because they had intended to serve a limited time until sufficient converts had been made to take their places. They then returned to the other Christian organizations which had loaned them for this groundwork.

Booth's insistence upon a definite decision for Christ out-and-out consecration to His service was so strong that no one could be comfortable under his leadership who was not prepared to go all the way with him in applying these principles to work which he felt so strongly they were called. The sifting out of the objectors and fainthearted was necessary. What remained were earnest and consecrated workers who stood by William Booth through thick and thin. Those who became a part of the work later did so with full knowledge of its standards and methods; and in fact, this is what attracted them. [1]

How did the early desertions of workers affect William? The records show that he just went to work more vigorously, seemingly undismayed. He wasn't dependent on numbers; his source of help and strength was the Holy Spirit.

He had already figured out that if he was going to attract the wayward, it wouldn't come through "churchy" music. His people were repelled by the lovely sounds coming from church organs. What they understood and enjoyed came from the twanging banjo, the mellow guitar, the blaring trumpet, and the big bass drum."

As the Christian Mission became known as The Salvation Army, branch missions were established in various cities and were named corps. Uniforms were designed, and ranks and titles were given just as in the military.

One early morning in May 1878, Reverend William Booth called one George Railton, his private secretary and his son Bramwell to his bedroom, to compare notes and receive instructions for the day. William was just getting over the flu, when he introduced the men to an eight page annual report of the mission. He called himself superintendent of A Voluntary Army. Bramwell the eldest child of eight, was twenty two years old and he objected to the wording of "Volunteer" on the material. He stated that he was not a volunteer, he was either a "regular or nothing." His father saw the sternness in his son and was a little shaken, immediately retrieved the pen from George Railton, crossed out volunteer and wrote "Salvation."

William's vision for The Salvation Army was:

[36.] "The distinguishing features are to be (1) authority, (2) obedience, (3) the adapted employment of everyone's ability, (4) the training of everyone to the utmost, and (5) the combined action of all."

William Booth spoke in London, in 1881 about the method that brought about The Salvation Army. He had tried several methods for eleven years, and after many plans, the movement took on the military form. William thought that God had ordained for them to have an army to deliver mankind from sin and Satan's power. The Salvation Army is called an "army of deliverance, and an army of salvation."

The Booths did not assume that education was unimportant, but many of their workers were uneducated men and women. There was a need for a greater number of officers so the Booths engaged a son and two daughters to train the cadets. Later The Salvation Army had and still has trained commissioned officers. These officers propagate the gospel, serve as: administrators, teachers, social workers, counselors, youth leaders, and musicians.

General Booth used his children extensively in the organization, one of his daughters, Evangeline (Eva) was in full-time service at the age of seventeen. She rose in rank from the lowest, a sergeant, to the commander of The Salvation Army in the United States of America. She was recognized by presidents such as Theodore Roosevelt, Taft, Wilson, Harding, Coolidge, Hoover and Franklin Delano Roosevelt; who all endorsed the work of The Salvation Army. As Helen continues to inform us:

> [37.] "Perhaps as much as anything, it was his own love and gratitude for his wife and what from the outset he observed she was capable of doing that influenced William. Early on Catherine was affectionately given the title "Mother of The Salvation Army." Every phase of their work bears testimony to her influence as the inspirer and sharer of William Booth's labors and leadership. Certainly the remarkable strengths of their daughters and daughter-in-law were influential in determining William's continuing high regard for the role of women.

Many people disagreed with The Salvation Army's official position that men and women should have equal roles within the ministry. Some people left the organization because of their objections to this position. But William and Catherine were not swayed. They were convinced that Scripture held God's sons and daughters in equal regard, and when William and Catherine believed something was in accordance with God's will, nothing would keep them from obeying.

One of the things that the general was fast learning, and that he then passed on to his officers, was that "it is in the interests of the service [The Salvation Army] to be in the columns of the newspapers—as often as possible." He has been inaccurately credited with inventing such eye-catching titles as "The Hallelujah Lassies," describing the women of the Army. Actually, the billing was the brainchild of William Crow, a Newcastle printer, who had been briefed to run off a handbill announcing the arrival of "Two Lady Preachers," Rachel and Louise Agar, on Tyneside.

Within days, however, results came flooding in to Whitechapel headquarters. Hour after hour brought more telegrams and inquiries, and no building on Tyneside was large enough to accommodate the crowds who came flocking to hear the Hallelujah Lassies. Miners and dockworkers, accustomed to calling their own wives "lassie," were curious and so anxious to hear more about this strange new religion that they rushed to come to the meetings. William Booth could hardly have guessed that the phrase would echo around the world, but he did learn an abiding truth from the "Hallelujah Lassies" incident: Any publicity that kept the Army's mission before the public and brought such results was good publicity.

From then on, William's soldiers took his injunction to heart. The officers were totally uninhibited, their methods as varied as what they sometimes wore. One man toured the streets as John the Baptist, barefooted, dressed in a skin hearth rug. East London Lass drew record crowds parading the streets wearing their nightgowns over their uniforms. Lieutenant Kitching, a mild-mannered Quaker who was also a schoolteacher, cheerfully rode into Yorkshire perched on a crimson-draped donkey. To advertise *The War Cry*, he borrowed the school's dinner bell and jangled it through the streets."

The first flag of The Salvation Army was designed by Catherine Booth. Although it had changed through the years, it still carries the stamp of the cofounder. At present, the flag has a dark blue border around a red rectangle, and a yellow star is in the center bearing The Salvation Army's motto, "Blood and Fire." The blue on the flag represents the purity of God; the crimson center, stands for the atoning Savior, and the fire of the Holy Spirit is depicted by the yellow star.

The Salvation Army had groups in several areas of the United States such as: New York City, Missouri, Philadelphia, Maryland, Ohio, Manhattan Island, Brooklyn and the Bronx. Many more workers came to work in America. There was an enormous need for assistance because

10,000 children roamed the streets of New York begging for assistance. The "East" side of New York was just a carbon copy of what William and Catherine dealt with in England because there were at least 290,000 people who lived in poverty in over populated areas. The Salvation Army marched through the streets flying their flags, and they persuaded many men to stop lying, stealing and cheating, and encouraged them to live upright lives in the future. Helen shares with us:

[38.] "As fast as they could, William and commander Railton marshaled forces to Germany, Sweden, Holland, Denmark, Zululand, Norway, Belgium, New Zealand, and South Africa.

Then there was India. No one was better qualified to lead salvation war into that country than Major Frederick St. George de Lautour Tucker, the powerful civil servant who had renounced all to join The Salvation Army. He was grandson of a chairman of the East India Company and a son of a judge in India. It was his work in India and the piety and faith he and his soldiers demonstrated that established The Salvation Army in that country on an unshakable foundation and made it an internationally respected missionary enterprise.

Tucker married Booths' beloved daughter Emma, on April 10, 1888. Upon their marriage he was appointed a commissioner, and Emma a consul. Together they pioneered work in India until 1896, leaving there when the climate proved too much for Emma's health. They were appointed to work in the United States and came to that work at a

critical time, just after Ballington Booth and
his wife Maud, left The Salvation Army."

Catherine was known as "Mother of The Salvation Army" although she
was never ordained, and never held a rank in The Salvation Army, yet
she was the most famous female preacher of her day. She was among
those who designed the uniform and was also instrumental in shaping
the doctrine and some of the methods of The Salvation Army. She was
fearless, and an advocate for the cause of women in the ministry. She
made salvation available to both women and men in the nineteenth
century, and established the fact that both men and women should
equally preach the gospel. She relied upon the leading of the Holy Spirit
for His empowerment to energize her as mother and wife in a ministry
that God entrusted to her.

In 1888, Catherine and William preached at several meetings, and she
complained to her eldest son Bramwell of a small painful swelling in
her left breast. She went to see the doctor, on the advice of her son and
discovered that she had a malignant cancer that had to be removed
immediately; her mother had died some years earlier from breast cancer,
and that was a long painful battle for her mother.

Catherine became very ill, and knew that it was time to say "so long"
to all. Although death was closing in upon her, her faith in God was
unmoved. She told them not to be concerned about her dying, but only
continue to live well so that they would die in Jesus Christ. Although
Catherine's illness progressed, she lived for another two years. Catherine
was unable to attend The Salvation Army's twenty-fifth anniversary
celebration in 1890 but she sent them a message:

39. "'*My Dear Children and Friends,*

*My place is empty, but my heart is with you.
You are my joy and crown. Your battles,
suffering, and victories have been the chief
interest of my life these past twenty-five years.*

They are so still. Go forward! Live holy lives.
Be true to the Army. God is your strength. Love
and seek the lost; bring them to the blood. Make
the people good; inspire them with the Spirit
of Jesus Christ. Love one another; help your
comrades in dark hours. I am dying under the
Army Flag; it is yours to live and fight under.
God is my Salvation and Refuge in the storm.
I send you my love and blessing.

\- *Catherine Booth*'

On Saturday afternoon, October 4, 1890, death came perceptibly closer. No longer able to speak Catherine pointed to a text that hung above her children's photograph on a mantle shelf: *My grace is sufficient for thee.* Someone took it down and placed it near her on the bed, already draped with the Army flag. Her family was there, comforting her and each other, singing some of her favorite hymns. Each in turn tenderly kissed her. William Booth's grey lion's mane of hair was swept back, as he bent low, his lips on hers.

"Pa!" she cried, as his arms went around her. Then she died.

The family was for a time inconsolable. Booth-Tucker, one of her sons-in-law observed: "The anguish of bereavement is the necessary penalty of love."

As the news of Catherine Booth's death spread, telegrams, letters, and words of condolence and praise poured into the London headquarters of The Salvation Army."

General William Booth lived twenty-two years after the death of Catherine. Although his strength was drained because of her death, he wrote and published a book, "In *Darkest England and The Way Out*. He continued to defend the poor and assist them; he worked so tirelessly that they decided to send him away from England. General Booth traveled to Canada, the United States, Japan, Germany, South Africa, Australia, New Zealand, India, Denmark, Norway, Sweden and Switzerland. His travels were not purely for recreation purposes, but to bring vigor and strength to his plan, to bring the gospel to the world, and win souls for the Master.

On one of Williams' trips to the United States, he visited Washington, and President and Mrs. Theodore Roosevelt held a luncheon for him and his daughter Evangeline. General Booth shared with the president his trip to Japan and the worldwide work of The Salvation Army. General Booth met with emperors, presidents, famous statesmen, and educators. His main concern was to get them to assist in the work of The Salvation Army, in delivering those less fortunate or otherwise the poor, unfortunate people of the world. He was asked of kings, governors, and politicians how they could help to alleviate the suffering that people were living with each day.

William celebrated his eighty-third birthday with a huge celebration that was given to honor him. He addressed ten thousand people in May of 1912, at his last public appearance, he told them that he was going for repairs in the dry dock. At that time General Booth was bent and was almost blind, when he told the throng that he was going to fight as women were weeping, and children were hungry. He stated that he would fight for the poor girls who were lost, and yet they were on the streets, without the light of God in their souls. He was determined to fight until his last breath left his body.

William had surgery in his right eye and it left him without his sight. General Booth requested of the surgeon to remove the bandages from his eye because he was blind and could not see the light. He informed the doctor of God's care during previous storms in his life and that God would continue to take care of him. He had a cataract in his left eye and had not gone totally blind in that eye, but the light was diminishing. In late may 1912, he was totally blind in his left eye. Helen continues in her book:

[40.] "Even though he was sightless, the old general's eyes were fixed on those who so desperately needed help. The problem of the homeless obsessed him. "I want you to do more for the homeless men," he urged his son. "Mind, I'm not thinking of this country only, but of *all* lands."

"Yes, General," Bramwell promised. "I understand."

"The homeless women—ah, my boy, we don't know what it means to be without a home."

"Yes, General, I follow."

"And the homeless children, Bramwell, look after the homeless. Promise me."

And Bramwell promised. But Booth, even in sickness, managed to draw on his sense of humor: Mind—if you don't I shall come back and haunt you!"

The old soldier fought valiantly for his life for three more days, even though he longed for rest. Finally at 10:13P.M., August 20, 1912, William Booth went to be with his Lord. In the words of poet Nicholas Vachel Lindsay:

Christ came gently with a robe and crown
For Booth the soldier, while the throng knelt down.
He saw King Jesus. They were face-to-face,
And he knelt a-weeping in that holy place."

The International Headquarters was bursting with the arrival of staff on August 21, 1912. The only message that was posted in the window stated that the General had laid down his sword. The Salvation Army is now operating worldwide, and is supervised by trained commissioned officers. They spread the gospel and serve as administrators, teachers, social workers, counselors, youth leaders, and musicians. The Salvation Army is in 103 countries of the world and is preached by its officers and soldiers in 160 languages. The Bramwell Booth Memorial Hall is located in Kingston, Jamaica, West Indies.

Sojourner Truth

Belle was one of eleven children who were born to James and Betsy, slaves of Colonel Johannes Hardenbergh. Hardenbergh learnt English, but taught the slaves Dutch, so that he could control them. Those Dutch felt that if their slaves were unable to speak English, then they would be unable to communicate with the vast throng of people surrounding them. Some of Belle's siblings died while others were sold into slavery. Her parents were hard workers.

Dutch settlers came to the United States in 1626, and began to import slaves from Africa to work on their farms. The area that they settled in was known as New Netherlands. The British seized the settlement thirty-eight years later and named it New York.

Belle was the youngest child and her parents feared that she might be sold as a slave as well. Although Belle's ancestors were Africans, she heard that she was a descendant of the Mohawk Indians, and that was why she and her parents were tall. Belle was nearly six feet tall, and stood straight.

Belle's dad was called Baumfree, because he was strong; her mother was called Mau Mau Brett. Belle's parents taught her how to be obedient and have a good deportment. They were aware of the harsh punishment that would be meted out to her if she did not obey. They also gave her lessons on working hard, honesty, and faithfulness. These parents taught Belle how to suffer and be silent; never making a fuss in the presence of white folks.

Colonel Hardenbergh died when Belle was only three years old, and his son Charles moved the slaves and livestock to another area in the hills. Charles had moved into his new home and there was no accommodation prepared for the slaves, so they dwelt in the cold, damp cellar. There was little light that came in during the day, and when it rained the water turned the floor into mud. In winter the slaves huddled together to keep warm, and in the summer the cellar was smelly, hot and humid.

Belle's parents were faithful and very loyal to their master, so he gave them a plot of land on which they planted corn, tobacco and other crops that they bartered with their neighbors for more food and clothes. Mau Brett soon had a son, and although the children were young she talked to them about God. W. Terry Whalin wrote in his book Sojourner Truth, American Abolitionist:

[41.] "One night when both children were still very young, their mother took them outside and told them to sit under a tree. "My children," she said to them, "there is a God who hears and sees you." The two small children looked around them, but they couldn't see God.

"Where does God live?" Belle asked her mother. "He lives in the sky," their mother answered, "and when you are beaten or cruelly treated or fall into any trouble, you must ask His help, and He will always hear and help you."

Clinging to the promise of a powerful guardian in the sky, Belle faced the difficulties in her life with increased confidence. This confidence continued to grow as Belle grew older and learned new things. On Sundays, Belle and the other slaves didn't have to work in their master's orchards or fields. Belle learned how to row a boat and ride a horse. Her mother taught her to obey her master, to recite the Lord's Prayer every day and never to steal or lie.

One night, Belle heard her mother crying. "What's wrong Mau Mau?" she gently asked. "I'm groaning to think of my poor children." Mau Mau said. "They don't know where I be,

and I don't know where they be. They look
up at the stars, and I look up at the stars, but
I can't tell where they be."

Later her mother told Belle how, many years
earlier, Michael and Nancy, Belle's older
brother and sister, had been snatched from
their family."

Belle's mother related the story of how her brothers and sisters were
taken away. Her mother feared that Belle would be snatched away from
her in the same manner. Charles Hardenbergh died in 1808, when Belle
was eleven years old, and his heirs decided to auction off his property
including the slaves. Belle saw the crowd of people at the auction and
she was scared, because she did not want to leave Mau Mau.

There was a thirty year old law in New York that stated that slaves over
fifty years old should go free. Belle's parents were now free but the dad
was too old to work so her parents remained in the cold damp cellar.
Mau Mau continued to work, while Baumfree was crippled in his
legs and hands with arthritis. The family spoke Dutch, Peter and his
sister Belle were placed on the auction block. Now Mau Mau is really
bereaved of her children although they were still alive. Mau Mau prayed
to God that He would see that her children were treated properly. They
all said their gut wrenching goodbyes.

An out-of-town man purchased Peter. It was Belle's turn and nobody
wanted her; she was unable to fathom what was being said in English.
The auctioneer was desperate to sell her, so he offered a flock of sheep
with her, and a John Neely, a shopkeeper purchased her, because of the
good bargain. Neely's wife was discontented because Belle spoke no
English.

Belle had a difficult time with Mrs. Neely because she did not understand
the English requests, so she was beaten regularly. Mrs. Neely got very
frustrated, so one Sunday morning she sent Belle to the barn where

Mr. Neely was waiting with his metal rod that was heating. He tied her hands, tore off her shirt and beat her mercilessly until she fell to the ground, after pleading with her master to cease. Belle was covered over with her own blood, so she crept into the woods and cried out to God for His help. God answered her prayer instantly.

Belle learned some coping skills and scrubbed the floors so that Mrs. Neely had nothing to complain about, but she still screamed at her. Belle began to learn English. She began to worry about ever seeing her family again, when one winter her father arrived at the Neely's home. Dad looked very old and sick, but he shared the events that were taking place at the Big House, with her. He said that they were still staying in the cellar, her mother was working, but they could not afford clothes and food.

Baumfree noticed that the deep snow was on the ground, but his daughter was not wearing warm clothes or shoes. Belle listened to all of her father's woes and when he was about to leave, he hugged her, and she pulled back in pain. As he walked to the gate, Belle followed in his large footprints in the snow. She showed him her scarred back, and that made him very angry that he was unable to protect his little girl. He vowed to use his freedom to free his little daughter. Terry's book continues:

> [42.] "Unfortunately for Belle, change took time. She continued working for the Neely family. After about two years with the Neelys, God answered what Belle later called a "desperate prayer." Somehow Old Baumfree persuaded Martin Schryver to purchase Belle from the Neelys for $105. The fisherman didn't own any other slaves but had a farm and a tavern on the Roundout River. This new location was only about five miles from the Neely farm.

Belle worked hard for her new owner, partially from gratitude but partially from fear of receiving another beating. The Schryvers were a coarse and uneducated couple, but they weren't cruel. They spoke both English and Dutch, so Belle could easily talk with them. Without someone yelling at her constantly Belle's English became more fluent.

The Schryvers treated Belle well, although sometimes she felt uncomfortable around the coarse men who frequented their tavern. A hard worker, Belle hoed cornfields, hauled in fish, and gathered roots and herbs for the homemade beer sold in the tavern. She had a great deal of freedom to roam outdoors. Occasionally watching the many white-sailed sloops on the Hudson River, she was startled to see one of the new steamboats throwing up black smoke."

Belle was fourteen years old, and yet she was six feet tall. She had a warm shawl for winter, and her master's hand-me-down shoes, for women shoes were too small for her feet. Mau and Baumfree Brett were sick because they could not afford enough food. Mau Mau died first, although she was younger than her husband. Belle and Peter were both able to attend the funeral.

Belle could not assist her sick, hungry father, but she prayed that God would show her how to assist him. One night Belle was working in the tavern and overheard stories about slavery, and abolition, so she wanted to know more about abolition, if she were free she could assist her father. Belle soon received a message that her father had starved to death. Belle begins to "understand her call." According to Terry:

43. "After Mau Mau's death, Baumfree had been allowed to continue living on the Hardenbergh estate along with two other slaves. But soon the other slaves died, and Baumfree was left in the cellar alone too sick to care for himself. Baumfree lived his last few months cold, filthy, and forgotten.

When the Hardenbergh family learned of the old man's death, they donated a pine box and a jug of whiskey for mourners. It was their final tribute to a man who had been a faithful, kind, and honest servant.

Other than Peter, Belle had no known immediate family still living. She felt alone, and God seemed so distant. In her own determined way, Belle decided to pray for the only thing left: her freedom. She remembered the words of Mau Mau about the great God in the sky: "God is always with you. You are never alone."

One day a man entered the tavern and when he saw Belle he inquired about her. Her master explained that she was only fourteen and was expected to grow well over six feet. The man said that she would work well on his farm, so he offered three hundred dollars for her. The Schryvers had planned to free her at the age of eighteen but Mr. Schryvers could not allow three hundred dollars, a lot of money in those days, to escape him. John Dumont took his new possession to his farm in 1810, and placed her with ten other slaves.

The other slaves explained to Belle that Mr. Dumont did not believe in administering harsh punishment or in separating families, but his wife was the opposite. Her tongue and temperament were destructive.

Plainly, she was to get out of Mrs. Dumont's presence, but that was impossible because Belle worked part time in the Big House. As Terry continues to share:

> [44.] "Mrs. Dumont pulled the two white maids aside and told them, "Isabella should be taught a lesson. Make sure you grind down her proud attitude."

> Despite the harsh treatment from her mistress and coworkers in the Dumont house, Belle remembered her mother's lessons on obedience, so she always tried hard to please her owners. Sometimes the other slaves chided Belle saying, "Girl, you're too obedient for Master and Miss Dumont."

> Throughout her childhood, Belle had been taught to repay evil with good. She had developed a deep belief that her hard work would eventually be rewarded."

It was one of Belle's duties to wash and boil potatoes first thing in the morning, but each time she did this chore Mrs. Dumont would enter the kitchen and complain that Belle was cooking the potatoes in dirty water. It was no use explaining that she had washed the potatoes, so she spent a longer time scrubbing them before cooking them. Mrs. Dumont still inspected the pot and complained about the dirty water, that the potatoes were in.

The Dumonts had a ten-year old daughter, Gertrude, who liked Belle. That night when Gertrude had the chance, she called Belle into her room and informed her that she surmised that Kate was doing the "dirty job," because she disliked Belle. Gertrude devised a plan to catch Kate. Belle was astonished at a white person doing a good deed for her.

Belle washed the potatoes as usual the following morning, put them to boil, and went to milk the cows in the barn. Gertrude was in hiding when she observed Kate entering the kitchen and emptied a clump of ashes in the pot. Gertrude came out of hiding, called to her, and went to inform her parents. Gertrude cleared Belle's name.

Belle mistook Mr. Dumont for a god and thought that he knew everything, so she worked so hard that she fell from exhaustion. She then told him everything and even reported on the other slaves. Dumont bragged about how Belle could work hard, and that made the other slaves call her names, and alienated her from their group of friends. No one understood what made her confused or hurt.

One day Cato the driver took her aside and scolded her. He asked her why she worked so hard, and told her that their master was going to expect the same from them. They were going to die without being freed, and that they would not have time to care for their children. Cato was the slave-preacher and he gave Belle an understanding of how he thought God worked, or answered prayer. Belle began to understand, then, that her master was not a god, but she had a great God in the sky to talk to. She was less confused.

Belle met a handsome young slave from a nearby estate, and it was love at first sight for this teenage girl. They began to date and could not be legally married because they were not citizens. Robert's owner objected to the relationship and because he was selfish he wanted Robert to take a girl from his estate, and have children to build his fortune.

Robert continued to see Belle, so his master and his son set a trap, and caught Robert who was visiting Belle one afternoon. They were beating him with heavy sticks under Belle's kitchen window, so that she had to ask her master to intervene and stop them from killing Robert. Belle watched Robert getting his beating and was then taken away in chains. Belle slipped away for a few minutes, prayed, sang the songs of her African grandmother, and cried very hard. She dried her tears, went back to work, and she never saw Robert again.

Dumont decided that Belle should marry a man by the name of Tom. Belle requested that a preacher marry them and the request was granted. Tom looked old and he was not standing straight. Belle noticed scars on his back and neck and was told that he had lost his young bride. She was sold to a family in the New York City some years earlier. He ran away to find her and stayed away from the Dumont's' farm for a month with some freed slaves. Tom never located his wife, but some slave trackers found him and brought him back and he was whipped severely.

Belle and Tom loved each other, and Belle cared for her husband. Their union produced five children: Diana, Elizabeth, Hannah, Peter and Sophia. Belle sometimes had to strap a child to her back as she hoed a field. She would tie an old sheet to a branch in the form of a hammock, place the child in it, and had the older children watch that child. The slaves at the Dumont farm assisted each other with child rearing.

Belle continued year after year to work hard, but she had the goal of becoming free one day. She got some good news in 1824, that the abolitionist groups forced New York State Legislature to pass an emancipation law. Slaves who were born before July 4, 1799 should be freed on July 4, 1827. Terry's book continues:

> [45.] "Male slaves born after that date were to gain their freedom when they turned twenty-eight, and female slaves were to be freed after their twenty-fifth birthday.
>
> Belle struggled over the date of her birthday. No one was certain of the exact day but the Dumonts agreed that Belle would be eligible for freedom in 1827. The slaves looked forward to what they called "Freedom Day." Even though three years stood between her and Freedom Day, just the idea of freedom put a bounce in Belle's step. She sang while

she worked and kept her sight unswervingly on freedom.

One day in 1825, Dumont came to Belle with an offer for her freedom. He complimented her on her hard work for the past fifteen years. Two more years remained until he was required by law to set Belle free.

'I'll let you go a year earlier than the law says I need to, if you promise to work extra hard for me," Dumont said. "And as a bonus, I'll let Tom go free with you and you can live in the cabin that I own down the road.'

Belle accepted the offer. Over the next several months, she put in the extra-long hours of hard work—planting, washing, cooking, and cleaning. Then in the spring, Belle cut her hand on a blade of a scythe. Because she didn't slow down and care for the wound, it didn't heal properly."

Belle continued to work hard, although the wound bled and hurt. Belle had fulfilled her promise to Dumont, it was now a year, but Dumont did not say anything to her. She could not wait for her freedom anymore so she ran to his house and confronted him. Dumont got angry, told her that the deal was off and she should return to work. Belle was upset and asked Dumont why he had changed his word and he gave her a lame reply. He informed her that because of her lame hand she could not have done reasonable work, so the fury burnt in her and she decided to run away.

Belle gathered her five children from ages twelve to less than a year old and her husband one early fall morning and told them how Dumont had cheated her out of her freedom. She assured them that she was going to run away, but that she would be back for them. Tom tried to dissuade her, but to no avail.

She could not leave in the daytime and she was afraid of the dark night, so she prayed and God gave her the answer: she should leave at dawn. Belle tried to be safe so she did not disclose her plans to her husband and children. Belle got a few things, wrapped up baby Sophia and left the rest of the family. She knew that the other slaves would care for the other children. When she was far from her mother's home she had to pray for the next direction.

Belle then remembered a Quaker by the name of Levi Rowe who spoke to her about the injustice of slavery. Rowe lived down the road from the Dumont estate so she decided to visit him. He had gotten older and he was ill, but he listened to her and sent her to a Quaker couple, Isaac and Maria Van Wagener. She walked to their home and realized that she had known them since she was a child. Dumont showed up and threatened her to punish her harshly for running away by night but she told him that she had walked by day.

Dumont tried to scare Belle but she was determined not to return with him. He then realized if she returned she would not work as hard as before. Then as the Van Wageners watched they saw that Belle was determined not to return so Mr. Van Wagener decided to pay twenty dollars for Belle and five dollars for baby Sophia. Dumont was satisfied. Belle thanked Mr. Van Wagener and addressed him as her new master but he corrected her and told her that she was free. Terry continues to impart to us:

> [46.] "Through the winter Belle worked for the VanWageners. The kind and gentle couple welcomed her in all ways. They lived simply, without a lot of frills. Often they sat for hours meditating on the Bible and praying—never saying a word. Such a life marked a sharp contrast to the storytelling and constant chatter in the Dumont slave quarters. On the

Dumont estate, slaves never went to church or read the Bible.

Although content to stay with the Van Wageners, the thought of losing her children tempted Belle to return to the Dumont estate. Years later, Belle told friends that a powerful force turned her around whenever she tried to leave.

"Jesus stopped me," she explained simply. Her spiritual experience was so powerful that Belle never again seriously considered returning to her old master. Freedom Day, when all of the slaves would be freed, was getting closer every day.

But Freedom Day didn't arrive soon enough. One day, Belle learned that Dumont had sold her only son Peter to a Dr. Gedney. The new owner planned to take the boy to England with him as a body servant."

Belle went to the Dumonts to have her boy returned, but she got only insults and was called demeaning names. She approached the Dr.'s mother, and she was rude. She treated Belle in the same manner as Mrs. Dumont and drove her out of her presence. Belle had a long struggle, but she did not give up especially with the help of the Quakers; she could not stop fighting for her son. God opened a door and she entered and although the six year old boy was threatened, and was told to lie to the judge, Belle got her son. He had scars in his face and terrible marks on his back. Belle gave God credit for sending His angel to help to release Peter. She vowed to get all of her children free.

Belle did not realize that she was one of the first black women in the United States of America to win a court case. Belle became a member of the AME church, the oldest African American organization in America. She was known for her spirit-filled prayers as well as singing the original hymns. Belle was thirty three years old and was looking for someone educated and in touch with God to guide her. She met Sophia and Michael a few Sundays later, and they informed her that they were her siblings, children of Mau Mau and Baumfree. She was informed that Nancy, her sister, was living in New York but had died recently. Belle realized that one of the elderly mothers who had prayed along beside her was her sister.

Belle was now an Evangelist with Mrs. Geer, Peter, and others. Later Belle traveled so much that she assumed the name, "Sojourner." She told her friends, goodbye and stated that she must be "about her Father's business."

During one of Belle's travels she stopped at a Quaker farm and requested a drink of water. The woman who gave her the water asked her for her name and she replied, "Sojourner." The woman then asked for her last name and she replied, "Sojourner," and departed. She then thought about last names and told herself that only slaves did not have last names. She asked God for a last name as she thought about the previous names that she had: Hardenbergh's Belle, and Dumont's Belle. The Scripture came to her from St. John 8:32, about knowing the truth.

Belle had just one Master and He was her God. She knew that His name is "Truth" so she called herself "Sojourner Truth." She was determined to walk in the Truth from that day forward. She went wherever God led her. She preached everywhere she went, even to white farmers. Although she was illiterate she caused them to wonder at her speech, and her knowledge of the Bible. News of this fiery preacher spread throughout Long Island.

Once someone asked her to speak about her life as a slave, and that was her first time speaking to a large group of white people about the evils of slavery. That was not her last either, because she continued to address crowds of white people for the rest of her life. She told this first group of her parents and eleven children who were separated, and some of the evils that they encountered. Terry reveals the following information:

> [47.] "In 1846, Sojourner made a trip back to New Paltz so she could visit her daughter Diana, who continued working for the Dumonts. While Sojourner was visiting her daughter, she was glad to hear John Dumont, her former master, repent for his past actions. He told her, "Slavery is the wickedest thing in the world.""

Sojourner spoke to many important people in her lifetime, but President Lincoln was her most famous admirer.

President Abraham Lincoln signed the executive order on January 1, 1863, ending slavery in the rebel states. The president proclaimed that everyone who was held as a slave within any state or the designated part of a state should rebel against the United States and be free forever. Those in North America cheered in tears when they received the Proclamation. Churches were ringing their bells and people were dancing in the streets.

Sojourner collected her friends and they cheered, sang, and gave long speeches. The people cheered and were joyful for the people who brought about their freedom. Sojourner had a stroke several days after the Emancipation Proclamation, and news spread that she had died. The editor at the Anti-Slavery Standard believed what he had heard and printed a story regarding her death. Author Stowe wrote about her meeting Sojourner, as a tribute to her life.

There were people who had never heard of Sojourner, but when they were introduced to her great work they were amazed. Someone called her the "Lilyan Sibyl (African)," which means that she was a prophetess from former times. Stowe could not fathom how an illiterate former slave had such intellectual abilities. She wondered how powerful she would have been if she had learned to read and write.

Sojourner was not dead as they supposed and she recovered speedily. Harriet Stowe was astonished when she received a letter from Sojourner expressing her gratitude. After the Emancipation Proclamation, black soldiers were allowed in racially segregated units. These soldiers in the North were happy to be enlisted, so at least fifteen hundred of them joined the 1st Michigan Volunteer Black Infantry. Injustice was meted out to these black soldiers, they were paid less than the whites, and were even mistreated by them. Sojourner spoke out against the unfairness, and asked why blacks were dying equally and were not paid equally for being alive. Her own grandson, James Caldwell was missing in action.

Sojourner went to Camp Ward, which was an army base and assisted the soldiers. She brought food that was donated by residents of Battle Creek, to feed the soldiers so that they could enjoy a good Thanksgiving dinner. She spoke to the men about being patriotic and they gave her a resounding cheer after her speech. She remained with the men and they sang a hymn that she had composed for the Michigan Infantry.

Sojourner appreciated President Lincoln for abolishing slavery, although some of her abolitionist friends did not share her view, they thought that the President had taken too long to abolish slavery. She was accompanied by her grandson, Sammy Banks to Washington D.C. to see President Lincoln. Sojourner did not let opportunity slip by her during her travel to Washington, she stopped in various towns to give speeches. She reached Washington D.C. in September, 1864, and upon seeing the American flag she said to her grandson:

[48] "'No more scars and stripes, just stars and stripes for all God's children.'

Parts of Washington reminded her of the Five Points district in New York City. The streets of Washington were filled with slaves who had poured into the city after their freedom. They lived in unhealthy conditions and were surrounded by despair and filth. Sojourner's heart went out to them, and she helped them whenever she could.

Freeing the slaves had created another problem: What was to be done with the millions of people who had no education or money and only limited skills? Congress had set aside funds to establish the Freedman's Bureau, which was designed to help freed slaves make the transition from slavery to freedom. Sojourner hoped that there might be some job for her within the Bureau.

When Sojourner learned that her good friend and former traveling companion, Josephine Griffing, was in Washington, she went to see her right away. Griffing had become the local agent of the National Freedman's Relief Association. When Sojourner expressed her concerns about the condition of the newly freed slaves, Josephine said, "I know just the place for you. Freedman's Village."

Constructed by the army as a model village, Freedman's Village was a series of neat cottages, a great improvement over the shacks the slaves had lived in during slavery. The village was located in Arlington, Virginia, just outside Washington, on the old estate of General Robert E. Lee."

While Sojourner was in the village, she assisted other women learn how to sew, cook, clean, comb hair, and care for their children. Sojourner traveled around as a younger woman, half her age. She made it possible for her grandson to attend school, as well as other children, and mothers were encouraged to attend adult classes.

Miss Truth discovered some women bunched together, terror-stricken and crying, she found out that some white men had stolen their children and forced them to work without being paid. Sojourner reminded them that they were free and should not allow anyone to take advantage of them. She assisted the women to utilize the law to get back their children. One of the white men was daring, trying to intimidate Sojourner with threats, he even had the nerve to address her as "old woman." He informed her that if she did not mind her own business they would imprison her. She responded to his intimidation, by informing him that if he tried what he had stated she would cause the entire Unites States to rock like a cradle, so they left the village and ceased from stealing the children.

Sojourner was in Washington for several weeks and had not met the president, so she asked a white abolitionist to arrange an appointment for her to meet President Lincoln. Miss Coleman, the abolitionist was an admirer of Sojourner, because she stated that she had never dishonored her (Sojourner) name, so she was willing to assist her.

The women got to the White House, and as they awaited their turn, Sojourner was pleased to observe how the President treated his black guests respectfully, and equally as he did the white visitors. Although Sojourner spoke to several important people in her lifetime, this encounter with President Lincoln would be "the icing on the cake," because she admired him very much.

Well, it was Sojourner's turn to speak with President Lincoln, she had planned to speak to him about the poverty that the former slaves were experiencing, but looking at his weary, tired face, she had a change of heart. She felt sad as she looked at the great man who had given freedom to the former slaves. Terry pointed out:

> [49.] "After she had sat down, Sojourner told him bluntly, "I never heard of you before you were put in for president."

Lincoln laughed at the comment and replied, "I heard of you years and years before I ever thought of being president. Your name is well-known in the Midwest."

President Lincoln showed her around his office and pointed out a Bible that a group of Baltimore blacks had presented to him. She held the book in her hands and traced the big gold letters—The Bible—with her finger. Although Sojourner couldn't read the Book, she knew many of the words in it by heart.

Remembering one of her favorite Bible stories, Sojourner reminded President Lincoln that he was like Daniel in the lion's den, but with God on his side he'd win, just like Daniel. Then she told the president that in her opinion, he was the best president that the country had ever had.

The president objected to her opinion saying that Washington, Jefferson, and Adams were greater. "They may have been good to others," Sojourner replied, "but they neglected to do anything for my race. Washington had a good name, but his name didn't reach to us"

Then Sojourner thanked the President for his efforts to help black Americans and advised him not to worry about the blustering attacks of his critics. The people in the nation were behind him and would support him in the upcoming election, she said. Lincoln in turn thanked her for her encouragement. When it was time to leave, Sojourner asked Lincoln

to sign her "Book of Life." For Sojourner,
the "Book of Life" was a combination
scrapbook and autograph book. Throughout
her travels, she collected the signatures of
the great people she had met and respected.
Also she kept personal letters and newspaper
clippings. Everywhere Sojourner went, she
took her "Book of Life" with her.

She watched with great pride as the president
signed, "For Aunty Sojourner Truth, A.
Lincoln, October 29, 1864." (Years later, the
terms "aunty" and "uncle" became words that
black women and men resented. During the
time of Lincoln, however, they were terms of
endearment."

December 12, 1865, Sojourner and millions of other Americans
celebrated what was known as the ratification of the Thirteenth
Amendment to the Constitution. Slavery had ended officially. After
the assassination of President Lincoln, Sojourner met with President
Andrew Johnson. He asked her in a polite voice to be seated, but she in
turn asked him to sit down, then she explained that she was accustomed
to standing because she had been lecturing for many years.

Sojourner told him of her concerns for the conditions that the people
were facing at the Freedman's Village. Sojourner had her "Book of
Life" but did not ask him for his signature. Soon after meeting Andrew
Johnson, she was assigned to work at the Freedman's Hospital. She
could be heard down the halls of the hospital instructing them to be
clean. She gave the best medical care to the blacks.

One day Sojourner was accompanying a black nurse to the Freeman's
Hospital and they took a streetcar with two white women aboard. The
women were full of hate for the Negroes. They inquired of the conductor
if "niggers" should not have had a car on the track. They thought it a

disgrace to ride with blacks. Sojourner's strong voice interjected that a streetcar was for poor whites and colored, but carriages were for ladies and gentlemen. The women left in a rage to take a more expensive ride. Terry notes that:

50. "'Ah!' Sojourner said, 'now they are going to take a carriage. Goodbye, ladies.'

A few weeks later, Sojourner and her white friend, Mrs. Laura Haviland, were boarding a streetcar together. Sojourner stepped ahead of her friend, but the conductor snatched her out of the way. 'Let the lady on before you,' he snapped.

'I'm a lady, too,' Sojourner snapped back. The conductor pushed Sojourner off the streetcar. Mrs. Haviland stopped the man. 'Don't you put her off,' she said.

'Why? Does she belong to you?' the conductor said angrily.

'No,' Mrs. Haviland replied. 'She belongs to humanity.'

'Then take her and go!'

The conductor slammed Sojourner against the door and bruised her shoulder. After Sojourner asked Haviland to jot down the number of the car, the conductor left them alone. "It is hard for the slave-holding spirit to die," Sojourner reflected, "but die it must."

Back at the hospital, when the two women asked a surgeon to examine Sojourner's shoulder, he found it was swollen. Then the two women reported the incident to the president of the streetcar company. He promptly fired the conductor.

This company president also advised Sojourner to have the conductor arrested for assault, which she did with the help of the Freedman's Bureau who furnished her with a lawyer. A few days later, Justice William Thompson held a hearing for the conductor, as reported in a curious article published in at least four Washington newspapers.

Sojourner won her case in court. As she said about the incident, "Before the trial was over, so many blacks were now daring to ride in the cars that the inside of the cars looked like pepper and salt." Soon the conductors who had cursed Sojourner for wanting to ride would stop for both black and white ladies and even condescend to say, "Walk in, ladies." Sojourner later claimed that her Washington ride-ins had changed the city. The old warrior marked another victory in her struggle for equality."

News traveled again that Sojourner had expired or become too old to travel, but she came back in public in 1877 looking healthier. She began to encourage the oppressed. She was blessed with better hearing and sharpened eyesight, her grey hair had turned black and her skin was almost wrinkle free. She spoke in thirty-six different towns in one year at this ripe old age. She became a delegate to the Women's Rights Convention in Rochester, New York. She spoke to newly freed slaves.

At the close of a tremendous journey, the tireless pilgrim was thought to be 114 years of age but her gravestone said she was 108. God's wonderful soldier understood her call and gave her life to a worthy cause. Although she could not read or write she had made history.

George Muller

George Muller had no religious experience when he was young, so he lived a life without any thought of God or morality until one day he found out that he needed God in his life. This sinful young man discovered God as someone who is great and could do more than he could ask or think. After God revealed Himself to him, he began to depend on the Lord, for his needs to be met. George was fully aware that God was dependable, and whatever resources man had, was just like a spot to the vast resources of God. He learnt that he could go boldly to God's throne, to receive what he desired. He placed his faith in the Lord. George would trust God for his daily needs and that trust lasted for seventy-three years. God was always available to meet George's needs, so when he asked for anything he knew that he would receive the same.

Because of George's trust in the Lord, and God's constant supply according to his faith, George was known as *the Apostle of Faith*. George was so sinful in his youth, but had an amazing transformation; it would seem as if God had made him all over again. George lived for ninety-three years, eight months, and walked with the Lord for seventy-three years, two months.

George was born September 27, 1805, in Kroppenstedi, in the Kingdom of Prussia, Germany. His father was a tax collector. George's father taught the children worldly doctrine, gave them money according to their age, and both children began their life of sin. George began stealing the government's money before he was ten-years old. One day his father grew suspicious of him, counted some money and left it in the room where George was, leaving him by himself with the money. George took the bait like a mouse caught in a trap, but he hid the money that he stole under his foot, in his shoe.

George's father found out that the money was short, searched him and found the loot. He was punished but that did not deter him from stealing the government's money. He continued to steal the money but never learnt how to hide his trick, because he was not smart enough. Between ten and eleven years old he was sent to Halberstadt in preparation for entering university, as his father thought that he should be trained for Lutheran ministry. This thought of his father was intended to give him a comfortable living, but not for serving the Lord. George indulged in reading and studying novels that taught him sinful customs.

George was fourteen-years old, his mother was dying, he was unaware of her illness, so he occupied his time playing cards, and the following day, which happened to be Sunday, he went drinking with his buddies. He drank as a youth and continued his life of sin. Basil Miller shares with us:

> [51.] "His mother's death made no lasting impression upon him. Three or four days before his confirmation, which admitted him to partake of the Lord's Supper, he committed a gross immorality. So deceitful had he become that he could not play square with the minister who confirmed him. "I handed over to him only the twelfth part of the fee which my father had given me for him," he remarks, delineating the downward course of his sins.
>
> 'In this state of heart, without prayer, without repentance, without faith, without knowledge of the plan of salvation, I was confirmed, and took the Lord's Supper, on the Sunday after Easter, 1820 . . . Yet I was not without some feeling . . . I made resolutions to turn from those vices in which I was living and to study more. But as I had no regard for God, and attempted the thing in my own strength, all soon come to nothing, and I still grew worse.'"

George did not consider God in any of his dealings, so he grew worse each day. His father was away once and he collected the government's money, and used it for his sinful pleasures. George spent the money like the Prodigal Son that is recorded in the Bible. He lived in an expensive hotel, but his money was finished so he tried to escape through a high window. This sixteen-year-old boy thought that he would obtain mercy from his creditors when he confessed to them, but to his dismay, he found no empathy. He was arrested, and thrown in jail as a common criminal.

George was incarcerated with common criminals and murderers, and was treated as they were treated. On George's third day in prison he requested a Bible from the keeper, just to keep him occupied, and not for any reverence, or because of interest in God's Word. He spent twenty four days in prison until his father paid his debt, paid for his keep in jail, and money for his trip home.

George went to school for two and a half years at Nordhansen. He cared not in the least about God, but continued in sin, then he got sick, and was caged in his room for thirteen weeks. George had a habit of taking the Lord's Supper; he abstained from sin the day before the Holy Communion, got very serious on the day, but after a day or two he returned to his former lifestyle.

He was given money by his father and would squander it. He had no money so he lied by breaking the lock on his trunk and guitar case, then he reported to the director that someone stole his money; his story seemed true. He got the desired response.

When George was twenty-years old, he became a member of the University of Halle and had the opportunity to preach in the Lutheran Establishment. He had to act as a clergyman should because they would not employ him in the church, and he was there just for the pay. My pastor related a story recently. He saw an advertisement on a city bus that caught his attention, so he took a close look. It was an appeal for prospective priests. There was a website given for interested persons to apply. He was very surprised to see a church advertising for priests. Priesthood is a holy calling and not a job to be taken lightly. Well, George went in for the wrong reason, for money only.

George is now a divinity student and he had no sorrow for the ways in which he offended the Lord. One day he met another student by the name of Beta, who had tried to live a Christian life. Beta, a backslider, tried to befriend George in order to learn his unholy tricks. Although George hated Beta, he decided to become his friend, so that his conduct would change. The two young men did not know that God had brought them together in order to transform Muller.

George became seriously ill again. Beta, George and two other students borrowed money to travel. George's evil ways resurfaced when they borrowed money on their books, and other possessions, using forged and false letters from their parents to obtain passports. Basil wrote:

[52.] "Wickedness was so inground in George's system that even on this trip he was a common thief. "I was on this journey like Judas," George confesses, "for having the common purse, I was a thief. I managed so that the journey cost me but two-thirds of what it cost my friends . . ."

But those sin-darkened days were near an end. God in His inscrutable manner had planned a meeting where the divine hand should begin remaking the life that sin had marred. The same Beta, with whom he had sinned, was to be God's instrument in bringing George into the glorious light of the Gospel. Sin's night was almost over and the daydawn of grace was about to burst with transforming beauty over the youth's soul."

All through George's youth he had never seen anyone kneeling and praying. He never knew the blessings that came from answered prayers, but when he observed the first man kneeling, his career changed.

One afternoon when George was twenty-years-old, he took a walk with Beta, who invited him to accompany him to a cottage meeting. Beta was in attendance at these Saturday evening meetings in the home of a Christian. George asked Beta what they did at the meetings, and was informed of the Bible reading, singing of hymns, prayers, and the reading of a sermon.

George realized that that was what his heart was searching for all of his life. He accompanied Beta to the meeting. George saw the joy that the Christians shared with each other, as they spoke and shared the things pertaining to God. He made an apology for coming, but the host informed him that he should come as often as he could, because the house was open to him. The earnestness of the group as they prayed, sang and called upon God, as well as the kneeling, brought about a change in George Muller that would last his whole life.

[53.] "When the benedictory hymn had been sung, the believers again went to their knees, to be led this time in prayer by Wagner.

"I could not pray as well," thought George, as he listened to the tradesman's eloquent pleas, "though I am much more learned than this illiterate man."

He was truly happy for the first time in his life. "If I had been asked why I was so happy, I could not have clearly explained it," Muller notes long after he had learned the joy of praying.

Homeward bound George said to his friend Beta, "All we have seen on our journey to

Switzerland, and all our former pleasures, are as nothing in comparison with this evening."

At home again the young man fell upon his knees. When it came time to sleep, George said "I lay peaceful and happy in my bed."

He had little doubt that God began a work of grace in his heart, a deep sense of joy springing up with scarcely any sorrow or with but little knowledge. The work of divine grace had been done and hence forth the young man is to walk the path of the just which shines with ever-increasing brightness until it ends in the perfect day.

His was a changed life. He read the Scriptures and not the classics as formerly, praying often, and attended church as prompted by divine love within. At the university he stood on the side of Christ, and gladly paid the price of being laughed at by his fellow-students for his religious fervor."

In January, 1826 he became a missionary after reading missionary papers, and meeting with a young man who was a missionary in Poland, working among Jews. George had God's peace at last, so that he wrote his parents entreating them to become friends of Jesus and have the happiness that he was experiencing. His father responded with an angry letter instructing him to stop the foolishness and become a clergyman to support them in their old age.

At last George decided to free himself from his parents, by stop taking their money, and place his faith in God for his needs to be met. His first provision came in the form of money paid to tutor some Americans who needed to learn the German language. He then preached his initial sermon that brought in more money. The Lord was really "showing up" for George Muller.

The young man attended a Sunday meeting with some religious students, the group grew from six to twenty. He came in contact with an orphanage and later designed his own orphanages. He resided in famous Orphan Houses for two months, and these were free, furnished for divinity students. A.H. Franke built the orphanages, more than a hundred years earlier just by depending upon God for sustenance and support. After Franke died the work continued through faith in God.

Muller began to follow Franke's footsteps by praying for God's assistance, and when he heard about a Continental Society in England's plan, to send a Missionary to Bucharest, he prayed about it and accepted the challenge. Twenty-two year old Muller received his father's consent to go, and after much praying God divinely intervened so that the work was abandoned because of the war. That was not God's plan for George.

Later George was asked by a Dr. Tholuck if he was interested in being a missionary to the Jews, and he was placed with the London Missionary Society for promoting Christianity among the Jews. After connections were made for the young missionary, the Society decided to place George as a missionary for six months. Muller's name became famous throughout the English speaking nations of the world, he was England's apostle of faith. As Basil Miller continues:

[54.] "There was a formidable obstacle. Every Prussian man must serve three years in the army; and classical students who had passed the university examinations were forced to serve only one year. Muller had not yet received his army training, and without an exemption he could not obtain a passport to leave the country. His application for exemption was denied, and Muller felt much depressed because of the denial. But God had plans for this exemption.

While in Leipsic with an American professor for whom he was serving as tutor in German, between acts at the opera George took some iced refreshments which caused him to become sick. This resulted in a broken blood vessel in his stomach. Being advised by friends to go to Berlin, he found an open door for preaching to wards in the poor house and in the prisons.

On February 3, 1829, he was re-examined for the army, and because of his stomach trouble was declared physically unfit for service, and hence exempted. Immediately, he received his passport and set sail for London where he arrived on March 19."

Muller was not accustomed to reading his Bible, but he read books about the Bible and now God was teaching him about His Word. He was taught that God's Word alone is the standard of judgement, and that the Holy Spirit alone can explain the Bible, so he then devoted his life to the Bible alone. Muller realized that the few hours that he locked himself away in his room with his Bible were more beneficial, than the months that he spent reading other materials. He gained strength for his soul as he spent time with the Bible.

Muller's love for God's Word made him comment before he died that he read the Bible through about two hundred times, one hundred of which, he spent on his knees reading it. He learnt to believe God's Word and to trust what he read. God was now ready to bring him to a place where he had to depend solely upon him.

Muller started prayer meeting for the seminary students, and after the services he spent time in the presence of the Lord. He began to distribute tracts, taught Sunday School for Jewish boys, and read the Bible to them.

Muller was waiting on the Lord, so he began to preach, and he was speaking on baptism when three ladies began to speak to him on the subject. They asked him if he had been baptized, and he said that he did not need to be baptized again. The ladies went further to ask him when he was baptized and he responded that he did it when he was a child. They asked him if he read the Scriptures and prayed about it. One of the ladies instructed him that he should refrain from speaking about baptism until he got baptized. He read the Scriptures and he subsequently got immersed.

When Muller first reached England, he heard of a Mr. Groves, the Exeter dentist, who was earning an excellent salary, but gave it up to become a missionary. He then met Mary Groves, the missionary's sister, courted her for a short time, then married her, and their union lasted for more than forty years, with many orphans who called her "blessed."

After Muller's marriage he informed his congregation that he would not accept any salary from them, because his trust was in the Lord. He informed them that they should place a box in the chapel, and if anyone felt like leaving a donation, he or she could. He and his wife were impressed to sell all they had and gave to those in need, and they complied. They began to lean on Jesus, to supply all their needs. Basil Miller explains:

[55] "Tests of faith were soon to come, as they came throughout Muller's long Christian career-trek; but he leaned heavily on the Master's strong arm, knowing full-well that if God clothed the sparrows, fed and housed them, he would not forsake him. This was to be a walk of faith and not of sight, and

the servant was to learn the lesson of trust through the school of experience.

The year 1831 was to be one of testing Muller's faith, for many times there was not a single shilling left in the house, though at the proper moment faith's reward came in the form of money and supplies.

One morning when their money had been reduced to eight shillings (about $2.00, a shilling equaling approximately 25¢), Muller asked the Lord for money. For four hours the preacher waited but still no reply. Then a lady came to the house.

"Do you want any money?" she asked.
Faith was tested, yet remained triumphant, and the minister replied, "I told the brethren, dear sister, when I gave up my salary, that I would for the future tell the Lord only about my wants."

"But," she replied, reaching for her purse, "He has told me to give you some money," laying in his hand two guineas.

Once the minister's faith was anxious when he saw a brother open the chapel box, for he was in dire need of money. He would not ask the brother for what came in, since he often stated in the pulpit, "I desire to look neither to man nor the *box*, but to the living God," Muller resorted to prayer, asking the Lord to incline the man's heart to bring the money. Shortly the box money was given him,

amounting to one pound, eight shillings and
sixpence.

God was gradually leading the young
minister to test His promises and see whether
they were true."

There were many times when there was no bread for the next meal for
the orphans, but God sent bread just in time. Once they did not have
enough bread for the day and after dinner George returned thanks, and
asked for their "daily bread," and simultaneously, there came a knock
on the door of the room, and after he finished praying, a sister brought
them some of her dinner, and another poor sister brought five shillings,
she brought a large loaf of bread as well. The Lord sent bread and money.

Muller did not believe in storing up money, he thought that that was
not consistent with faith. He also believed if money was given for one
purpose, then it should be used to meet that need and nothing else.

Mr. Muller stated that the only highway that leads to the throne of God
is prayer. He encourages us to pray patiently, believe and continue praying
until we obtain an answer. We are not only to continue in prayer unto the
end, but we must believe that God hears us and will answer our prayers.

Mr. Muller was a man of giving; giving himself unto prayer so that
God may meet the needs of his own family and also the large family of
orphans he was caring for. He believed that since God gave him gifts
through faith, he should also join the group of faithful givers. God
had instructed him to open his mouth and ask for what he needed, he
had no fear in asking God for the supplies he required to do his work.
Continuing, Miller informs:

[56.] "These donations came to him through
faith alone, and he recognized that he must
be the channel through which God's gifts
should flow out to others in need. He looked

upon himself as the Lord's steward. What money he received he believed should be given rather than hoarded.

A crippled woman, who through the years was a constant though a small giver to the orphanage work, expressed Mr. Muller's philosophy of *living* and *giving*. She began giving a penny a week out of her earnings towards the care of the orphans, and the Lord blessed her so much that she was able to raise her weekly gift to six shillings, or a dollar and a half. One gift she wrapped in a piece of paper, on which she had written: *"Give; give; give—be ever giving. If you are living, you will be giving. Those who are not giving are not living."*

The total amount Mr. Muller gave away out of his private funds amounted to approximately $180,000 from the year 1831 to November, 1877. This it must be recalled came out of a poor trustful man's penury. He had only what he prayed in from day to day.

The Fifty-ninth Report of the Institution, issued May 26, 1898, immediately after Mr. Muller's death, reveals a very interesting item concerning their servant's method of giving. Year by year in the annual Reports there were frequent entries of gifts *"from a servant of the Lord Jesus, who constrained by the love of Christ, seeks to lay up treasure in heaven."*

Mr. Wright, who succeeded Mr. Muller as head of the Institution, checked those entries,

and found that this servant had given up to
March 1, 1898, the aggregate sum of *eighty-
one thousand four hundred and ninety pounds,
eighteen shillings and eight pence.*"

Mr. Muller stated that many of God's children lose out on privileges
and blessings because they refuse to give to the needs of the poor. He
used the passage of Scripture of 'giving to the poor, and lending to the
Lord' to respond to someone's questions. The Man of Faith explained
that when we give, we must give to the Lord and not to man. Although
man may be the recipient, but when the humble heart gives gifts, it must
be because of the blessings of God upon the body and soul of the giver.

Mr. Muller believed that acquiring gifts for God's work should be done
in God's way. He did not believe in asking unbelievers for gifts for the
Lord's service, neither did he think believers were to be pressured into
giving. He believed that the duty and privilege of contributing should be
stated, followed by earnest prayer, believing, and it will result in giving.
No man should state his trust in God, when he has a store laid up for
future wants, because the Lord will send him to that supply that he had
stored up, before answering his request for more. Muller thought that
all that he owned came as gifts from the Lord to be used for His service.

God supplied the Muller's needs from various quarters, and in all kinds
of descriptions. He received money from different sources, large sum
that amount to thousands of dollars, and even a penny. He received
bread and shoes. Some people sold their furniture and gave the money
to him to do God's work. Mr. Muller received thousands of dollars
worth of jewelry that was sent to be sold for the ministry. The gifts
continued to pour in, in various sorts for the work: autographs that were
given to be sold, a silver medal, a horse-car, and a lady's original hymns
to be published. When there was a pressing need, Mr. Muller called a
prayer meeting with his staff, and quite often as they got off their knees,
wagons would be backing up to the kitchen door with buns, bread,
apples, cakes, potatoes, soap, peas, venison, rabbits, pheasants and all
other sorts of food items. Mr. Muller's gifts began with a shilling from

a poor missionary to start the orphanage until his last entries of gifts in March, 1898. God supplied all types of persons and gifts, small and great for the work of the ministry.

Mr. Muller was as strange a man as strange people came. One night he conducted his last prayer meeting and then gave the last hymn, said goodnight to his son-in-law, and went to bed. The next morning when the servant took a cup of tea to his room, a usual custom, she saw him lying on the floor. He had requested a glass of milk and said that it should be placed on his dressing table. While he was having the biscuit, he must have fallen, and the doctor was called, but he was already dead. He died on March 10, 1898 at ninety-three years old.

Muller had stated that God had answered fifty thousand of his prayers, many thousands of them were answered the very day he prayed when he got up from off his knees. He had started to pray for five persons in November 1844, and he prayed every day, without stopping. After eighteen months, the first of the five got converted, then after five years another one got saved. As he continued to pray for the other three, there was a six year span when the third was converted. He thanked God for the three, but the other two remained unconverted.

Two sons of a friend were unconverted and he interceded for them for fifty-two years, every day. After he died God saved them.

An old lady who attended George's funeral was one of his first orphans, sixty years prior to his death. Mr. Muller was buried in an ordinary area, a slope of a hill, under the shade of a yew tree, beside his first and second wives. He cared for about ten thousand orphans. Mr. Muller's staff continues to trust God for their needs and He who never fails us, meets the needs as at the start of the work.

Gladys Aylward

China was receiving missionaries in 1928 when General Chiang Kai-shek became President. Gladys wanted to go to China as a missionary. She was attending a theology class at the Women's Training Center of the China Inland Mission in London when she was summoned to see the center's Principal.

Gladys waited with trepidation; different thoughts were flooding her mind. As she anxiously waited on the principal to arrive she trembled as to how pitiful she looked. She then asked God's forgiveness for the anxiety that was overwhelming her. She heard some footsteps approaching, she prayed to God as the principal sat at his desk.

The man began to speak coldly to Gladys who tried to explain her past record at her former school, but he interrupted her to explain that the instructors were dissatisfied with her performance. He also stated that she was far behind the other students and she required a period of three years to be prepared to be the missionary that they normally send out. Gladys instantly replied that she would remain the three years to prepare for the mission, she was told that she would be too old, at the age of thirty. The principal then interjected that everyone there thought that her age would prevent her from learning the Chinese language.

Gladys was about to respond, but the reply died in her throat. She was thinking on David Livingstone who was twenty-eight, when he became an expert in Bechuana, South Africa; and Mary Slessor was about the same age when she mastered the Efik language in Nigeria. They were both nearly thirty years of age and took control of those languages. She began to think that her dream of becoming a missionary to China had died right in front of her eyes. There was a turmoil that was boiling over in Gladys' mind as she recalled the preparations she made through the pastor's wife. The words that she heard were like a frozen dagger in her heart.

The principal suggested other ways that Gladys could serve in England, but she refused them all. She was heading back home and she began to recall John Wesley's trip on the same route that she was traveling, with disappointment. She also remembered that George Whitefield was as an angel that met John and changed his life and Britain forever. In his book, Gladys Aylward, Missionary to China, Sam Wellman captures the information in this manner:

[57.] "From a refined, even dandified, Anglican Church pastor Wesley became a preaching firebrand of the outdoors—and Britain was never the same again. But who was meek Gladys Aylward to compare herself with John Wesley?

"You must learn to trust God with all your heart and soul, Gladys," urged the male half of the retired missionary couple in Bristol after she arrived. "You came here to Bristol with doubt in your heart. Listen with your heart and mind and He will give some sign." "But how." "Read your Bible. Pray with fervor. Talk to people who serve Christ. Serve Christ yourself!"

Bristol was not joy or fulfillment for Gladys, but it was certainly enlightening. Under the elderly couple's sagacity she began to learn about the real China too—not the rosy images painted by the China Inland Mission to recruit missionaries, but the blackness of the real China: the throwing away of girl babies like trash, the binding of women's feet into crippled clubs, the sickening arrogance of men taking more than one wife. The plight of women in China was an abomination. And the condition of men was not much better.

This old couple had seen it all and they didn't mind telling Gladys about it.

Did they do it to harm the missionary effort? Not at all. "Quite the opposite!" stormed the old missionaries.

Gladys knew exactly what they meant. The horrors of China demanded the love of Christ. And it was the wife who soon sized up Gladys and told her about herself. "You've too big a heart to waste on just two old fools who think they are righteous anyway. We're going to find you a spot where you can help the lost."

"Yes, we'll not slow this young warrior down," added her husband. "She must move on!"

Whether it was the old man or the old woman or Gladys who arrived at the conclusion Christ would be better served by Gladys moving on into "Rescue" work was hard to say. Certainly Gladys herself, except for the privilege of hearing the missionary couple talk about China, thought she was wasted in Bristol. But all three were so immersed in local evangelism as well as correspondence everywhere—yes, Gladys too, because she read and wrote letters for them—that it was hard to know when or how or from whom the city of Swansea beckoned Gladys."

Gladys left Bristol to Swansea, that was about fifty miles away, and that was like being on a foreign mission. Swansea was in Wales, where sailors from all over the world gathered. Gladys worked at the Sunshine Hostel, she was to rescue drunken women, because the men were too large for her. It was even worse when they were drunk. She sought for the very young women who had just arrived at Swansea. She brought them back to the mission-hostel, where they got sobered and were placed in beds. It happened that the following day they returned to the previous day's behavior. She tried to assist the older women, but the thought of China kept haunting her, so she was thinking of how to get there on her own.

Gladys was employed by a very influential family in London. She accepted employment with the Younghusband family so that she could save money for her trip to China. Sir Francis Younghusband traveled widely and he visited China as well. Gladys was happy for the chance to use their library to gain more information regarding China.

Gladys began to study her Bible like never before. She felt God speaking to her from her Bible. She began to "field preach" on the sidewalk away from the Younghusbands' home. She made certain she stayed away from popular areas where their great Rolls Royce would travel. She stayed on Hyde Park telling men and women about Jesus. She worked for her employers and preached when she was free. Sam continues:

[58.] "Invariably she stopped in Hyde Park to preach on Fridays. That was the day she also rushed along Piccadilly to the Haymarket where Mullers' Travel Agency was located. For there Gladys was making payments on her fare to China. They hadn't wanted to sell her a ticket at all.

"But you don't understand, Miss," the travel agent had groaned. "Train travel to China by the overland route through Russia is not possible right now." He became truly obstinate only after he decided the commonness of her clothing took precedent over her superior accent.

"But I can't afford seafare," she countered logically. "It's twice the cost of a rail ticket."

The travel agent patiently explained why she could not take the train from London to Hull, take a ship across the North Sea to The Hague in Holland, then take the train all the way across Russia, then continue on through Manchuria to the port of Dairen on the China Sea. There a steamer would take her to the Chinese port city of Tientsin, he said, if she made it to Dairen, which she could not. The Chinese were fighting the Russians on the very border between Russia and Manchuria.

"I've heard of no such war," she objected.

"It is precisely over control of the eastern end of the railroad—the part that goes through Manchuria—that they are fighting," he emphasized. "Some Chinese warlord they call the 'Young Marshall.'"

"That would be Chang Hsueh-liang," she amplified.

"His name could be Chop Suey for all I care," he fumed. "The point is—there is fighting going on."

"I'm a woman," she told him logically. "They wouldn't hurt a woman."

"We do not want our customers—especially young women—to reach their destination dead!" he pouted.

"Please take this on account," purred Gladys, pushing some money toward him.

Gladys could tell the travel agent was biting his tongue. His face seemed about to explode. But suddenly his face softened. He had realized her down payment was a mere three pounds sterling. She would need fifteen

times that amount to complete payment
on a ticket. He studied her attire. She was
obviously in service somewhere. Even senior
servants earned not much more than about
twenty pounds a year. This Miss Aylward, he
must have been reasoning to himself, would
never be able to completely pay for the fare."

Gladys was determined to go to China and she was making her down
payment for the trip. It seemed as if it would take many years as the
agent estimated her salary for the year and the cost of the trip.

Some of the staff at the manor began to ridicule Gladys. Some said that
she was insane. Every one of the workers at the job thought that she
would never reach China. Some of her friends from other manors tried
to entice her with other entertainments to keep her from thinking about
the unthinkable, her taking a trip to China. Sam continues:

[59.] "Her few chitchats were with workers in
various church organizations. Some were
acquaintances from the China Inland Mission
Center. Some were acquaintances from other
mission societies. One day in early 1930 was
memorable.

"Poor old Jeannie Lawson, Glad," said a
friend at a Methodist Church auxiliary.
"She's seventy-three. The old missionary tried
to retire here in England last year but it was
too tame for her, I guess. The old dear felt
compelled to return to China."
"How interesting."
Her friend grinned. "One of Jeannie's friends
got a letter recently. The old dear is afraid no
one will carry on her work. Seems Jeannie is
begging for an assistant."

"Then why doesn't the mission society send her one?" asked Gladys, her heart pounding. "She's tried for years to get help. It seems the help must come not at all—or come unofficially . . ."

"That's me!" gasped Gladys.

"You might want her address then."

Gladys wrote Jeannie Lawson at once to offer her assistance. Then after much prayer she resolved to go ahead just as if Jeannie Lawson had already written back with her approval. This was surely God's plan for her, reasoned Gladys. And she must trust God. She applied for a passport. She changed her emphasis: There was no time to read about China now. No time to preach. Every moment must be spent raising money. She was far short of money needed for her rail ticket across Russia. She must put the word out that she was available for extra duty outside her manor.

It would surely help her cause to be employed in such prestigious manor. Sir Francis hobnobbed with bluebloods like the Winston Churchills and Lord Kitchener. Sir Francis knew personally world figures as diverse as Cecil Rhodes, Mahatma Ghandi, and the poet Yeats. So it was not hard to spread the word. If another manor needed someone to help with a party, Gladys was available. If it was an all-night party, so much the better. Upper crust revelers glowing from a night of celebrating, paid best of all. If help was needed with a banquet, Gladys was available.

House work, kitchen work, garden work. Gladys was available."

Gladys began to act by faith. She started to sell her nice belongings, with the expectation that Jeannie Lawson would accept her as her assistant. One day the butler collected the mail and noticed one special envelope with an extra special stamp on it: to his amazement, it had writing that resembled Japanese or Chinese, and it was for Gladys. One of the maids announced that it was from China. Suddenly all the maids, the cook, the housekeeper, the lady's maid, the valet, the chauffeur and others gathered around Gladys and asked her to open the letter. She did not open it until she got to her bedroom. She did not know what to expect, so she was scared. Her fingers trembled as she finally opened and read the letter. The letter that contained good news.

Within a few months Gladys raised enough money for her passage to Tientsin where Jeannie Lawson had made preparations for someone to escort her to her final destination. When she was departing from the manor the staff was amazed that she was really leaving for China. On the day of her departure from the Liverpool Street Railway Station, her parents and Sister Violet were there to send her off. Her Brother Lawrence could not get leave from the military to be with the family.

Gladys was on her long trip to China. She experienced different cultures and practices as she traveled from one country to another. There were times when she misunderstood commands as she transferred from train to ship to trains again; she had quite an experience, but she was determined to reach her destination, China. On one occasion, she had to rest in a small tunnel in Siberia, where the winter was very unfriendly. She prayed to God for courage. She had to walk at daybreak from the tunnel that was her shelter that precious night, with the hope of not spending another night in Siberia. Unfortunately, she got to the train platform in the dark, so she slept outside in the Siberian winter, again, but this time there were Russians camping out there as well.

Gladys saw some Russian men gathering around her at daybreak, and she explained to them that she had purchased a ticket to Dairen on the China Sea. She explained that she expected to be taken to her destination whether or not the trains were running, if not she would settle with transportation by bus. Some soldiers later took her inside the station and pushed her in a small room. After informing them that she needed to go to China, they slammed the door in her face and locked it. An official came and spoke to her later, and because of the language barrier he locked her up again and she spent the night in the room. She had her tiny stove and a little food, so she made herself comfortable for the night.

The following morning she had a visitor who spoke rough English. She tried to explain that she was a British citizen and her brother was in the military. She spoke to him of other things, she even pointed to pictures in her Bible, finally she was placed on a train, north on the Sea of Japan. She encountered many difficulties from the Communists in Russia.

A captain of a Japanese freighter finally assisted Gladys so that she could get away from the Communists who were about to send her to a machinist work camp, where she would work as a machinist. They were going to lie that she volunteered. Gladys prayed constantly for God to protect her, and she praised Him as He helped her. The Japanese Captain finally bought her a train ticket and sent her on her way, he was eager to get her off his hands.

Gladys boarded a steamer at Kobe, that sailed out into the Pacific Ocean, but the Sea of Japan was not peaceful at all. One day Gladys discovered a distant land, and realized that she was nearing her destination, "China."

60. "Gladys knew Tientsin had been eagerly embraced by the British since the northern part of China—the China that revolted around Beijing—really opened up a corridor for trade in 1860. Before that time the only

five ports open for trade with China were much farther south.

So many buildings had been erected by the British that Tientsin actually looked European. It was a bit disconcerting to Gladys. Certainly this was not the quaint China of her dreams. Nevertheless the Chinese people themselves were from her dreams, maybe even from her unconsciousness, maybe even from Providence.

While riding in a rickshaw to the headquarters of a mission society she was startled to remember how disappointed she had been as a teenage girl with her own tiny stature and black hair—back when she still dreamed of becoming and international star of the stage. And here she was now among short, black-haired people. The similarity had never even occurred to her before. It was strange how the past tweaked her with no warning.

Gladys called at the mission society in Tientsin. "Jeannie Lawson said I was to wait here until she sent a guide for me," she told a woman missionary.

"Jeannie Lawson?" gasped the woman. "Oh gracious me, I don't think so. That could take a very long time. You see we would have to get in touch with her. Then she would have to get in touch with us and . . ."
"But . . ."
"You must just go on ahead and find her."
"Find her?"

"Yes, she is a bit of a renegade, you see."
"An elderly missionary woman?"
The woman smiled indulgently. "Jeannie Lawson travels around in the province of Shansi pretty much as she pleases."

The mission society took Gladys in, while they searched for someone dependable she could travel to Shansi with. In the meantime, she explored. She was quick to discover the Great Wall, which she would not see for many days yet, was in itself a real symbol for Chinese history. Walls were everywhere. Walls, walls, walls. Villages and towns were walled. The smaller villages consisted of one main street lined on both sides by walled buildings. So each building was a small fortress in itself. A visitor went in one gate of the village and went out the other. At night the gates were locked. The poorest of the poor lived outside the walls."

It was now Gladys' chance to learn the Chinese language which the principal at the mission in London informed her that she was too old to learn. She prayed that God would help her learn the language before she was thirty. The missionary informed Gladys that it was easier to learn the Mandarin sub-language which had less tones, and the listeners would understand what she was saying. She realized that written Chinese could be understood by only the educated people in China.

Mr. Lu, a Christian, escorted Gladys along her journey, on train, and on busses. Mr. Lu educated Gladys as a tour guide would enlighten a visitor. He told her of customs and the way of life in China. Once she told him that it would seem as if blue was the favorite color, but he explained, that it was the cheapest color. The dye came from a root that was found all over China.

Gladys noticed that the inn where they had lodged was an enormous guest room, with no privacy. Her guide explained that no one undressed, but if someone desired to do so, he or she did it under the blankets. Mr. Lu explained that it was a custom for Chinese to undress under the covers, even in their own homes. Gladys observed that everyone turned their shoes over and shook them out, before putting them on in the morning. Mr. Lu was unable to find an English word to explain why that practice existed. One morning Gladys noticed a scorpion falling out of a man's shoe—Gladys got her answer. She and her guide traveled for a month before they reached Tsechow.

When Gladys and Mr. Lu reached the mission, Jeannie was away in the mountains. One Mrs. Smith greeted Gladys. Mrs. Smith explained that Jeannie traveled from one village to another by mule, and a very old one at that. Mrs. Smith informed her that she, had been in China as a missionary for almost fifty years. She began to inform Gladys of customs that she needed to know. Sam Miller documents:

> [61.] "Gladys felt as if her brain was rattling around inside her head. The muleteer and his assistant had loosed the rear ends of the poles and the shanza had dropped like a rock to the ground. Gladys was going to complain to the men as they walked past her, then realized the front ends would soon be falling too. She scrambled out of the shanza.
>
> A woman as tiny as Gladys, dressed in blue robe and pants, faced her with her hands on her hips. The woman had snow white hair. Fierce sky blue eyes were not softened by small round "granny" spectacles.
> *"Chi-la-fan-ma?"* she asked

"Oh, have I eaten?" blurted Gladys.

"Well yes, chi-la, thank you very much for asking, but no, I haven't really eaten. I'm starved. Well, what I mean to say is . . ."

"English?" interrupted the woman. "Who would you be then?"

"Why, I'm Gladys Aylward. Are you Jeannie Lawson?"

"Well, of all the . . ." The woman brushed her question off as ridiculous. "You'll be coming in then," she said and scurried inside the building.

Gladys passed through the doorway and entered the courtyard. The building was two-storied, spacious and sturdy but very littered. Jeannie Lawson pointed at this pile of rubbish and at that broken door, chattering all the while as if Gladys had known her for a lifetime. Her accent was very thick. Gladys knew it was Scottish at one time. But this strangely accented English had been shaped by fifty years in China. Sometimes Gladys strained almost in agony to understand what Jeannie Lawson said, only to realize she was speaking Chinese.

"So this is your mission house?" mused Gladys during one of Jeannie Lawson's few pauses.

"Maybe and maybe not," replied Jeannie Lawson stubbornly. "I've just rented it. I could only afford it because the locals think it's haunted. I know you're burning up with curiosity to know what the rent is . . ."

"Why, no."

"Less than one pound sterling a year! There, now you know. Are you satisfied? Anyway, now that you're here we'll have it cleaned up in no time."

"Then it will be a mission house."

"Maybe and maybe not."

Gladys heard a commotion outside and wandered over to the only door that opened to the street. A ball of mud struck her shoulder and she heard a child scream— *"Lao-yang-kwei! lao-yang-kwei!"* and scuffle off. She turned to Jeannie Lawson.

"Lao-yang-kwei. They called you a foreign devil," sighed Jeannie Lawson as if it happened a hundred times a day. Gladys had read in Sir Francis' travels that the Chinese could be very hostile to strangers, but she had not wanted to believe it was true as a generality. But perhaps it was. *"Mu yu fadze,"* said Jeannie Lawson. She seemed to startle herself by speaking Chinese, so she quickly translated, "It can't be helped." She sighed again. "They are even more frightened of me because of my white hair. Very few Chinese have white hair. Be thankful those urchins couldn't find any stones.""

Jeannie educated Gladys on the life of a missionary in China. Gladys discovered that Jeannie suffered some form of old age disease, it was a form of senility. Gladys began to wonder what she would do if something should happen to Jeannie, because some of the natives ran from her, some spat and threw mud at her, while others called her a "foreign devil."

Gladys lived and worked among the people of China. She was in China when the attack on Pearl Harbor occurred. The Japanese had been attacking China for years, they were a constant threat to the Chinese. Gladys worked in several areas in China. Sam Miller explains:

[62.] "In 1945 she heard how the Japanese had returned to their own land and "fell on their sword," just as Annie Shaw had predicted from her Bible. Although war with Japan was over, war in China continued. Chiang Kai-shek's Nationalists were now fighting the Communists.

Could Gladys survive another tragedy? For five years now she had lived in tiny rooms, often with refugees. She had no private facilities. Like the poorest Chinese, she used outside latrines and washed up when she could. Her one luxury was a thermos bottle. In the morning she heated water to boiling and poured the steaming liquid into the thermos bottle. All day long she refreshed herself with weak tea. But it hardly sustained her. Pushing herself beyond her strength she still had blackouts.

She worked with lepers now. She was far more than a nurse or a comforter. She brought the hopeless the hope of Christ. Once the most miserable of human beings, her lepers now glowed with their love in Christ. Gladys persuaded a pastor to regularly give them the Sacrament of the Lord's Supper.

"Their bodies are so contorted with disease they cannot kneel," observed the American doctor Olin Stockwell. "Their hands are so crippled they can barely receive the elements. Yet their eyes flame with joy and hope. All because Gladys Aylward brought them to Christ."

Once Gladys trekked the heights ramping up into Minya Konka, a peak of Himalayan size only a hundred miles from Chengdu. There she had a mystical experience. She found a monastery hidden on the far side of a mountain, much as her old Bei Chai Chung had been isolated. The monks expected her! Here at long last was the messenger they had waited for, they said. They eagerly accepted her message of salvation through Christ. The whole episode seemed a dream after she returned to Changdu to work with the lepers and refugees again.

She taught English to eager young students. One pastor gave her a room in back of the church and a regular salary to be his "Biblewoman." For this she did every chore he asked, including cleaning the church building. Always she was busy. Everywhere she was a force.

She was also exasperating to less committed people. Only God and the Bible guided her. She could never account for any money given her. As likely as not she had given it away within minutes of having received it. Always her fellow missionaries tried to slow her down.

"It's not the work that is crushing me," she told cohorts. "It's the fate of my children. I heard my son Less was yanked out of school by the Communists and shot. He's not the only one of my boys who had died for Christ. And my daughter Ninepence is married but I don't know where she is. I don't know if she is alive or not."

Gladys had resided in China for seventeen years without leave. At this time there was much unrest in China and thousands were fleeing the country. Dr. Stockwell wanted Gladys to visit her loved ones in England, so he gave her some money. While she was awaiting her visa, she found Ninepence in Shanghai. Gladys was happy because Ninepence was now a mother, so she was a grandmother. Gladys finally reached England in 1949, and found her parents and siblings still alive. She could not adjust to life at her former address, she was tormented, lamenting over the poor of China. Gladys was asked to give a speech to the ladies' group in Hoxton, and was concerned about her English, but surprisingly it returned as she began to speak.

A journalist wrote about her life in China. A producer from the BBC took her experience lightly by saying that she had had adventures in China. The producer was informed that contrary to his belief, Gladys had worked tirelessly taking orphans to an orphanage in the mountains. The reporter was baffled.

Gladys was unhappy that her Chinese was not being used, so she went to help at a hostel where she used Mandarin to some Chinese seamen and refugees. She canvassed for cast-off clothing which she sent for refugees in China. Burgess from the BBC continued to interview her for four months. Burgess was writing a book about her life. Gladys could not recall the dates that events took place but she recalled her birthdate. While this was happening, her mother passed away and that affected her very much. Gladys was fifty years of age and realized that she had been in England far too long. She paid her passage to Hong Kong.

Twentieth-Century-Fox wanted to purchase the movie rights from her, she signed them over, and made a comment that she thought that they were foolish to pay good money for the story of "a little parlor maid."

Gladys got to Hong Kong and found that people were hopelessly trying to get out of that country. Gladys found out that people were streaming out of China into Hong Kong, but she wanted to enter her beloved country. She found one of her "sons," Michael who traveled through the mountains with her. Michael was at that time a minister so he, his wife, and Gladys devised a plan to begin a mission for refugees in Hong Kong. Gladys was a Chinese citizen so she was denied a resident visa.

Gladys' book had been published by Alan Burgess, "*The Small Woman*," and people were talking about it and the movie as well. Gladys was told that people enjoyed the movie. She continued to get reports about the movie. Some of the information she had given was changed. Ninepence was referred to as Sixpence, and they reported that she was her last child instead of the first child.

The movie caused millions of people worldwide to be aware of Gladys, so she was invited to the United States by World Vision, on a speaking tour. Many people expected to see a tall, beautiful woman, but instead they were introduced to a tired-looking middle-aged female who was wearing a Chinese gown. They were disappointed when they saw her, but as she began to speak, they were astonished at the message she shared. She raised funds for her work in Formosa. Gladys was invited to speak in Australia and New Zealand. She met the Archbishop of Canterbury, and Queen Elizabeth as well.

Gladys did not care about money for herself, she gave away to those in need as fast as she received it. She was cheated out of funds for her orphans. The movie did not portray her as it should have done. She trusted God who never failed her because human beings had failed. She then remembered a person of comfort, Annie Skau, so she sought her out in Hong Kong. Gladys was not very healthy so Annie invited her to refresh herself at her home.

Gladys cared for children among her other dedications. She was a dependable missionary who understood the call of God on her life. Sam concludes in his book:

63. "Back in Tapei she resumed her work, although it was more curtailed than in the past. Kathleen mothered her into less activity and better health.

"You must take care of yourself," insisted Kathleen.

Sometimes when Gladys reflected on her life—for at long last she had leisure time to indulge in reflection—she could not believe her own experiences. Had that been the parlor maid Gladys tumbling from the second floor of a Chinese inn after a bomb blast? Had that been Gladys dodging soldier's bullets outside Tsechow?

"How God rewarded me with adventure just because I was willing!" she cried.

In the first days of 1970, Gladys awoke with what she thought was a severe cold. In spite of Kathleen's protests, she kept a speaking engagement at a woman's club in Tapei. She returned to the orphanage so exhausted she tumbled into bed. Kathleen called a doctor, who determined Gladys had the flu.

Gladys's mind drifted to Nehemiah. Nehemiah, the servant, had always been her special Bible hero. It seemed that she too had restored a few walls, built a few gates. She too had resisted intimidation. But even Nehemiah's work was finally done.

"Oh God, 'spare me according to the greatness of thy mercy,'" prayed Gladys, quoting Nehemiah, but then she prayed her very last words, "'Remember me, O my God, for good'" Later that evening in January, Gladys Aylward, 67 years old and totally expended, joined the Lord."

Harriett Tubman

Jesus came to set people free whether they are black, white or polka dot, male or female, rich or poor, young or old. Although Jesus liberates Christians from their bondage of sin, the society can still enslave them. I realize that slavery has been abolished, but there are still slaves in our country and in our world. Some human beings are treated like beasts; some people in America treat their dogs better than they treat people.

In 1854 in Maryland, an older woman sat waiting for her grown children to return from the plantation. She and her husband roasted a pig, and prepared their favorite kinds of food. Those children never came although she and her husband constantly looked out the door for them. As she rocked back and forth, she waited and it was now dusk, she was unaware that her children were hiding in a shed filled with animal food, just waiting for it to get dark enough, so that they could flee from their lives of slavery.

Harriet, the youngest of ten children was born to this couple in their old age. She watched her mother through the open cabin door, but could not speak to her. Ben and Harriet Ross were unaware of their child's watchful eyes, and Harriet was able to see the old woman crying. Harriet had been secretly taking away slaves for five years. She was escorting them to freedom in Maryland.

They had planned to say, goodbye to their mother, but they realized that she would have gotten very emotional and others would have discovered their plans, endangering their lives and the lives of their parents. Harriet wished that they could celebrate Christmas together, but she thought that they needed to rest before embarking on their long journey to freedom. Their journey on foot would take them through Maryland, Delaware, New Jersey, and into Pennsylvania. Two men knocked on the cabin door and asked Poppa Ross for food. Poppa Ross stepped outside and the men explained that his children who were in the shed, needed food for their long journey and also wanted to say good bye.

Poppa Ross returned to the cabin and told Mrs. Ross what the men had told him so they prepared food for the travelers. When Poppa Ross got to the shed he asked the men to blind fold him and the friends thought that he had lost his mind. He again instructed the young men to blindfold him very tightly, and one man complied. Harriet and her brothers spent Christmas with their dad in the shed that night, and they talked together, but he never removed his blindfold. The group of travelers took some food and headed north. In her book, Free Indeed, Callie Smith Grant shares with us:

[64.] "Old Poppa Ross knew that when his children were discovered missing, he would be questioned, and Poppa was a devout Christian who would not lie. And sure enough, once the family members were discovered missing, he and his wife were called to the master's house which everyone called the Big House, for questioning. Slaves were missing in the area, so the authorities had come to question the Rosses about their children.

Of course, Momma Ross knew nothing. "I looked for them all day," she said sadly. "They never did come."
"Did you see your children before they left, old man?" the law asked Poppa.
"No," he said. "I ain't seen my children in months." And it was true. He had talked to his children; he had eaten with them. But he did not "see" them before they escaped to freedom. And he knew he might never see any of them again.

But meanwhile he had the great satisfaction of knowing that his baby daughter, now all grown up into the courageous Harriet

Tubman, slowly and with the assurance of one watched over by the Lord Himself escorted three more of Poppa Ross's own blood into the land of Canada. There they would be slaves no more. And one day Harriett was coming back."

Harriet Tubman led some slaves out of the South to freedom in the North. She encountered many difficulties as she brought freedom to many tired, hungry, feeble bodies. Well, the Bible tells us of a group of people who were slaves in Egypt, and God used Moses to deliver them from bondage. It was not an easy task, because he was threatened by Pharaoh, and some of the very people who he was liberating, but God delivered them all by His all-powerful-hands.

When Harriet was six years old, she was sold into slavery, at that time she was known as Minty Ross. Minty was on her way into slavery after she was pulled from the arms of her parents, by her former boss and owner, and now she was on a strange journey with a stranger. This family needed a slave but the only one they could afford was a child. After Minty left the comfort of her parents and the plantation she grew up on, she began to think what the neighbors would be thinking. They would be asking questions of her fate, with white people who had just snatched her away.

In the "bad old days of slavery," slaves in the south owned nothing, not even themselves. They could not travel as they chose, without permission, they could not move. They could not sleep when they were tired. They lived in one room shacks with dirt floors, without windows, and had to be satisfied with the little food that they received. The ladies had one dress and the men had a shirt and a pair of pants. They labored on tobacco and cotton plantations that made Southern planters very wealthy.

Slaves made attempts to get away very often, some were successful and others were less fortunate because they were tracked down by dogs and brought back to the plantations. They would often suffer harsh punishment and were sold to another plantation, shackled in chains.

Minty's name was really Araminta Ross. She had two older sisters who were sold to a chain gang when they were very young. Callie Smith Grant continues:

[65.] "No doubt there would be a grim future ahead of baby Minty since slave life was so hard. But the slaves themselves found ways to live their hard existence with a certain amount of joy. One way was their love and concern for one another, and another way was their love for God. Their sorrows, their hopes, and their aspirations—were expressed in worship to Him and in song.

On some plantations, slaves were allowed to gather for church. Other plantations found any gathering at all too threatening—the slaves, they feared, would be planning escape or, even worse, the murder of their masters. On those plantations, slaves would worship in secret in what they called brush arbors— areas of dense pine boughs that would absorb the sound. Even fear of whip did not keep them from praising Jesus out loud.

Today Minty looked up at the pearl-grey sky. She took comfort in the knowledge that her mother was praying for her this very minute. She'd heard her mother pray fervently in the privacy of their cabin every time a slave disappeared. Then she would rock and moan. It was kind of like singing, but it was softer, and it seemed full of all the hurt in the world.

> Today, at age six, Minty suddenly understood
> her mother's prayers and moans in a way she
> did not even the day before."

Minty began to think of slaves singing in their slave quarters that caused their masters to deem them as dangerous; because they assumed that the slaves were thinking evil thoughts. She did not see how singing about going to glory could be construed as being evil. Stories from the Bible that made slaves sing could not be bad, because slaves could rarely read. Minty's favorite song was about Moses leading the Israelites out of bondage in Egypt. They experienced many difficulties before reaching the Promised Land.

Minty knew that the song meant that Jesus would come one day, take His people away, and things would be better. She knew that vicious animals will lie down with gentle animals and will not hurt or destroy them, and certainly, there will be no slavery. Minty, though so young, knew that slavery was wrong. Some of the masters who were "Christians" read their Bible differently on the topic. Slaves knew that God did not intend for them to be made into slaves. She began to compare the song about Canaan with freedom in Canada. The Bible speaks of the Promised Land of Canaan regarding the Israelites. While Canada and the northern states in America had no slavery, in the southern states slave ownership was practiced. Minty finally reached her destination, a small log cabin with a river close by, far away from the Plantation of Brodas.

The Cooks were not wealthy people, Mrs. Cook was a weaver and Mr. Cook trapped fish and hunted animals. When Minty got to the cabin, she thought it was the biggest house that she had ever entered, because she was not privileged to enter the Big House on the plantation.

It was Minty's job to wind the yarn while Mrs. Cook worked the loom on the wheel. The poor child did not know about such hard task so Mrs. Cook would always harass her. Minty sneezed constantly because the fuzz got into her mouth and her nose. She was scared and homesick,

Mrs. Cook got upset with her and handed her over to her husband, so that he could work her. Mr. Cook taught her how to use the trap in the river.

One day Minty got the measles, but the Cooks made her work just the same. In those days children died of common, curable illnesses. The Cooks did not have any mercy on the child. She had a fever and had to walk barefooted in the cold river to pull in the heavy baskets of trapped fishes. Minty's fever got worse, and she developed bronchitis, along with the measles. Understandably, she collapsed, and the Cooks just wrapped her in a blanket, and left her unattended.

Although there were no telephones, internet or post offices in those days, the news reached the Brodas' plantation about the plight of the little child. The slaves in the slave quarters had juicy information even before the inhabitants of the Big House. Momma Ross beseeched Mr. Brodas to bring back her baby so that she could nurse her. Brodas begged Mr. Cook to return Minty and he consented because if Minty had died he would have lost his money.

When Minty arrived, her mother nursed her back to good health with herbs and food, then she was returned to the Cooks. Because of the bronchitis at such a young age, her voice was affected, it now sounded husky. Minty now had to stay indoors and work on the weaving. She could not manage and the Cooks would not feed her because she could not work. Eventually she was returned to Brodas with the tag of being stupid.

Seven year old Minty had her share of work on the plantation, but to be near family and playmates made life worth living. Her parents were concerned that she was too much problem to Brodas and he would probably sell her again. They thought that their youngest child was smart.

Brodas needed money to keep up his standard of living, so news was circulating around the plantation that he was about to sell another batch of slaves. Plantations were constantly selling slaves instead of crops, the chain gang continued to move slaves. Minty was not sold to a chain gang, but to Miss Susan, to do house work.

Minty a child, had to care for Miss Susan's colicky baby who cried a lot. Poor Minty had to sit on the floor, cross her legs and place the baby on her lap, all day until Miss Susan was ready to feed her. During the night the baby slept in a cradle while Minty slept on the floor. In fact she did not sleep because the baby was very fussy and she had to constantly rock the cradle. She learned how to rock the cradle and doze off at the same time.

Miss Susan expected Minty to care for her log cabin as an adult would. Minty was told to dust the furniture but she had no idea of what Miss Susan was speaking about, because she came from a dirt-floor shack, to the Cook's floor, near the ashes in the fireplace where she slept. Miss Susan a mean woman, would beat her and call her stupid. Miss Susan's sister had mercy on Minty, scolded her sister about beating the child, and then taught Minty how to clean a house.

Miss Susan would beat Minty if and when the baby cried. The moody woman constantly beat Minty. One day the child stole a lump of sugar, and Miss Susan whipped her, she could not endure the life of the whip and slavery anymore, so she ran away.

Minty got away from Miss Susan and her husband who tried to capture her. She lived in hiding and fed off pigs' food that she fought the pigs to get. She had no way of getting back to the plantation, so she returned to Miss Susan, and she was given a beating that left her bleeding. They then returned her to Brodas, and informed him that she was stupid. Brodas gave her to her parents, to heal her wounds, she had new wounds on top of old scars.

Her mother expressed her anger to Poppa Ross and to the Lord. She doctored Minty's back and neck, while Minty slept on her stomach. As Minty was healing and getting stronger, Brodas informed her mother that he was going to hire her out. Minty was not even ten years old, but Brodas hired her out as a field hand, for cash. She did not grow over five feet tall and yet she was very strong. She was skinny, but had muscles like that of a man. At eleven she decided that she was no longer a child, so she dressed like a woman and did hard work.

Minty sang songs with the workers, and she prayed and gave thanks, because her mother taught her how to pray. Although slaves were not allowed to converse, when the overseers were not close by, the slaves were talking, and Minty heard about the "Underground Railroad," she listened to stories of those who left, never to return. She began to think about trains running under the ground, until the constant whispers made her understand the meaning of the words. She heard about the Quakers who opposed slavery, because God made all men equal.

Minty learned all the information that would assist her and others gain their freedom. She was told that citizens who were called "conductors" assisted the runaway slaves to gain freedom. When Minty heard about white people who aided the slaves, she found it difficult to believe and trust them, because the people who beat her and sold her were also white.

Brodas called Minty "a good slave" although she was only thirteen years old, because she sang, worked hard and did not talk a lot. He could not read her mind and thank God for that. She realized that it was wrong for her and all the other people to be enslaved, and she was being pressured by the bondage that held them captive.

One day Minty saw a jittery slave and discovered that he wanted to get away, but she did not like how he acted in the presence of the overseer although he had his back turned to them. The man finally began to run, and the overseer chased him on foot because he had no time to mount his horse. Minty followed them into a building and the overseer ordered her to tie the man so he could whip him.

The slave ran pass Minty who stood there watching, the angry overseer picked up a two-pound rock and threw it at the escaping slave. The rock slapped Minty in her forehead and she fell in a pool of her blood. Her parents heard about it, took her home and placed her on a pallet on the floor where she was in and out of consciousness. She was at "death's door," quite often. She had a cracked skull and an ugly, dreadful hole in her forehead. She slept a lot and would be half awake sometimes but dozed off again.

When the other slaves heard of how she assisted a slave to escape, they changed her name to Harriet, her mother's name. With Momma Ross' herbs and prayers, Minty lived. The slaves began to wonder about her fate. What would Brodas do to her if she lived? If she survived and was unable to work as before what would happen to her? Momma Ross had to pray and work hard to keep Minty alive. Minty was unable to walk or speak, it was months before she regained consciousness.

Brodas found out that she was recovering, and tried to sell Minty, but prospective buyers only laughed at him. Minty had terrible headaches, and even the scar was painful. Minty now had a mental condition, where she fell in and out of deep sleep, and this took place during her daily life activities. If she was speaking, eating, walking, working or doing any other daily chore, she would fall on the ground, fast asleep, as if in a coma.

These sleep episodes brought visions to her, telling her how to be the "deliverer" of her people. She lay on her pallet praying that God would save Brodas, but unfortunately she did not know if he was saved, because when she heard that he was planning to sell her and her brothers to a chain gang, she prayed for God to kill him. She knew that she was not strong enough for the trip and she was too sick to run away. Brodas became ill and finally died. When she found out that her master had died she was penitent that she had prayed for him to die and he did, so she vowed never to pray for God to kill anyone again. She heard that her prayers did not kill him but she kept asking God for forgiveness. She also asked God to help her do good in the world.

After Brodas' death, his heir, a doctor as well as a minister decided not to sell any slaves outside of Maryland, for the time being, so the slaves' fears subsided. Harriet recovered and was doing housework, but her master hired her out to a man. She then requested of him to allow her to work outdoors. Harriet worked like a man, because she was as strong as an ox. Stewart, her new master used her to entertain his friends, by allowing her to haul a barge down the river, wearing a harness that was connected to the barge. She walked along the river side.

The boss Stewart allowed her to hire herself out, so she worked with her father, cutting down timber. Her dad taught her everything that he knew about nature. He realized that his daughter was too special, not to be a freed woman, so he was preparing her for the journey. Poppa Ross knew that he might not see his daughter again, yet he desired that she be freed, she sensed his thoughts. He taught her edible herbs, roots, and berries. He taught her which plants were for medicine, and how to use them. Poppa taught her about the river and marshes of Maryland, and all about the geography of Maryland. He was made aware of the information as he traveled with Brodas over the years. Poppa taught her how to move quietly in the forest. He taught her how to listen to sounds and how to interpret them. She was taught how to mimic the hoot of the owl and the sounds of birds.

She was now in her twenties, had some money and realized that she needed a husband. She was looking around for a suitable man, and at the same time John Tubman saw her and loved her, because he was a free man she thought that "he was the one." Harriet fell in love with John. They "jumped the broom" together and became man and wife. Slaves in those days did not have the privilege of having weddings like the whites. They gathered around a broom that lay on the floor and jumped over it.

Although Harriet was a slave, her husband was free, his parents' master had died, so they were freed; this happened occasionally. Harriet realized that she and her entire family were slaves and could be sold at anytime. She loved John, but if she was sold she would never see him again. She thought of the Underground Railroad. She wanted her husband

and herself to flee north, so she suggested to him that they should run away. John, who was always sweet, became upset and wanted to know why Harriet saw it necessary to become free. Harriet was shocked and inquired of him about her freedom and if they had children in the future, their freedom as well.

John told Harriet that they were content, because he had money and she could be hired out for money. She reasoned with John, who only shook his head. As Callie continues:

[66.] "Harriet started having a series of dreams at nights. In them, she could see and hear the terrors of slaves being rousted out of their cabins at night and sold. She could see and hear the chain gangs trudging, their irons clanking, the slaves weeping.
Then she dreamed she was swimming across a river. Just as she was about to go down in the deep water and drown, women dressed in white reached out, grabbed her flailing arms, and pulled her across.

She decided the first dream was a warning from God that she was going to be sold, and the second dream was a comfort from God, that she should head north, that His angels would watch over her. She approached John Tubman again about running away by telling him about the dreams.

First he laughed at her. Then he became angry. He bent down and put his face close to hers and said, "If you run, I'll tell the master." Harriet was stunned. "You know what they do to runaways," she said. "You would let them do that to me?"

"Try running and see," he said. She looked deep, into his eyes and saw no love there. For the first time, Harriet was afraid of John. This was a terrible hurt that her own husband would threaten to betray her to the master—a betrayal that could cost her very life.

But Harriet needed to be free. And she believed the Lord wanted to help her to be free, always had known it, and she believed that if John could see clearly, he'd want the same. She was certain that the time would come when he would see freedom as something his wife must have. But that time was not now.

Harriet became more determined to leave as soon as possible. Now she needed not only to watch for the right time to escape, she also had to observe John closely so that he would not know. She did not doubt for a minute that he would turn on her.

By 1849, enough time had elapsed without Harriet leaving that John no longer seemed suspicious. Harriet noted it and was relieved. But it wasn't yet time to leave.

One day a white woman approached Harriet while she was working in the fields near the road. Harriet had never looked at white people's faces much. In the south, blacks did not look whites in the eyes, and Harriet found their faces frightening anyway. They seemed to have no insides, no warmth."

The white woman and Harriet became friends, and she told Harriet that if she required anything she knew where she lived. They were both talking for weeks. Harriet could not remain in slavery any longer, and she could not tell her thoughts to John. She asked three of her brothers to accompany her because she was afraid to travel alone; her brothers decided to go with her.

John was asleep one night and she and her brothers left on their way to freedom. They traveled for a mile and her brothers decided to return, and they also encouraged her to return with them. She got back in her cabin without John's knowledge. Two days later, Harriet heard that she and her three brothers were going to be sold in a chain gang so Harriet had to leave, when it got dark.

There were many odds against her but she was determined to escape alone. Harriet left that night alone, but she knew that God was leading her. She had a sister working in the kitchen at the back of the Big House, so she passed by, composed a song and sang it to her, for her to know where she was, and departed. Harriet said goodbye to the first white friend that she had. The woman gave her instructions to assist her on her journey. God provided many people to assist her on her way to the North. There was a network of Christians who were strategically placed in the right areas to help her reach her destination safely.

Harriet arrived in Philadelphia safely. It was freedom at last. Callie wrote:

> [67.] "Since arriving in Philadelphia, she was meeting dozens of fugitive slaves, and she came to know the organizations that helped them upon their arrival. Harriet now realized that what a slave needed to get to freedom was courage, God's mercy, and the knowledge that it could be done. She wanted to help.
>
> More importantly, Harriet wanted every one of her family members with her to breathe

freely and walk where they wished and earn their own money to live the amazing freedom she was living. If she could make it, they could too! But they didn't know that, and they certainly didn't know how to go about it.

She decided to go back to Maryland as soon as she was able and spirit away her relatives. Maybe by now John Tubman would change his mind and come with her. Her heart leapt at the thought."

She heard of a free black man whose wife and two small children were in slavery, and the Volunteers who assisted fugitives in Philadelphia required a woman for the job, one of the children was a baby. As Harriet listened to the story she recognized the names of her sister Mary and her husband who were fugitives. The volunteer stated that they were about to be sold, and Mary required assistance with the children. Harriet volunteered and with the help of a Quaker friend, her family escaped slavery.

Slaves were being freed by those who had escaped its ugly hands very frequently, so that the Fugitive Slave Law was drafted by Congress in 1850. Slave owners had the right to travel North in an effort to track down their slaves, who they considered "their property." It became a crime to assist run-aways, even in the North where there was freedom. It was dangerous for the Underground Railroad. Harriet knew that it was her calling to free slaves and she understood it quite well. She knew that God was with her and He made her fearless.

Harriet realized that under the Fugitive Law a run-away slave would be returned to the plantation and be beaten savagely to teach him or her a lesson and others were also taught vicariously. The captured slaves would be sold and their lives, if they endured the harsh treatment, would be worse than before. Those whites who assisted the slaves were more angry than fearful because they were aware of the fact that they would never be owned, whipped or sold. They knew that the Law was immoral and was against the laws of God, so they felt no obligation to obey it. Some man-hunters from the South came to return run-aways but they were outnumbered by the angry townspeople, so some slaves were spared and sent to Canada.

Harriet was planning to go to Canada but she continued to travel to Maryland to escort three slaves, one of whom was her own brother. She went to visit her husband John; she knocked on the door and heard a woman's voice. John came out and she did not like the look on his face, it could not be trusted. He had a young, beautiful, woman with him, so she felt ugly and debased. John did not recognize her at first because she was wearing men's clothing and a hat. As soon as he peered down in her face under the hat and realized that it was her, he laughed, and she smiled.

John was informed by Harriet that she had come to take him back with her and the beautiful woman who was standing next to him began to laugh. John told Harriet that the woman was his wife, so feeling humiliated, she left them as John shut the door. Harriet cried softly in the woods, knelt down and prayed to God. She then knew that she must continue her mission of escorting slaves to freedom. People called her Moses, so when that hoarse voice was heard singing "Go Down, Moses" they knew that she was around to take them to safety. Although they did not see her, the throaty voice or the birds' call would alert them to leave. They left without making a commotion, but they would be missing in the morning. God directed her all the way by vision and other methods so that she "landed her passengers safely," she never lost one of them because the Holy Spirit was her Pilot, and Captain.

Harriet made several trips to emancipate other slaves. As Callie continues:

> [68.] "One time to get to her former plantation to spirit away more slaves, she disguised herself as an old granny with a raggedy dress and a scarf draped over her head to keep the sun off. She bought several live chickens, which she carried, then she slouched down

like a doddering old woman and hobbled down the road in broad daylight.

Of all people, who should ride up the road on his horse but her former master himself! Surely he would see the prominent scar on her face. Quickly, Harriet let go of the chickens so that they squawked and ran and half-flew every which way. Then waddling and bent over like an old woman, she chased after each one. The doctor watched for awhile, chuckling as he rode on."

"Sometimes a slave was too frightened or too exhausted to go on. But Harriet made him go on, for the sake of many. If he turned back, the law would find ways to make him talk, and the entire Underground Railroad would be jeopardized. Slaves would be sent back to slaveholders, and white citizens would be thrown into prison.

For these reasons, Harriet always carried a gun. She prayed never to have to use it, but when a slave threatened to turn back, she aimed the gun straight at the slave and said with absolute conviction in her voice "Go free or die." The slave never turned back. In all her years as a conductor for the Underground Railroad, Harriet never pulled the trigger of her gun."

Harriet began public speaking to groups informing them about slavery and the mission that God had given her to set slaves free. She told them of the Underground Railroad. There were times when she was speaking, and she lay right at the podium fast asleep; that did not bother her audience. She would wake up to continue where she had left off. She was a speaker who was in demand. She worked as a spy for the Union Army. She also assisted the Confederate encampment to rescue 750-800 slaves. Harriet worked in the hospital for the army throughout the Civil War. After buying freedom for herself, she made nineteen more trips for slaves.

Harriet brought freedom to over a thousand slaves. Her husband was not one of them, instead, she heard that he was murdered in Maryland. Harriet was known as "Moses" just like the deliverer in the book of Exodus in the Bible. Ninety-three year old Harriet, "Moses" died in New York, in 1913.

CHAPTER NINE

CALLED TO SERVE

Clifton R. Clarke

The author of Called To Serve states that for the past ten years he and his wife have been serving, in the areas of training missionaries, teaching theological students, and training pastors. He preached and taught both in Europe and the United States. He has also lectured, and finally he concluded that what has prevented the progress of church growth is a lack in successful tutoring, mentoring, and equipping.

Reverend Clarke related to a survey that showed that some ninety per cent of ministers concluded that the ministry was totally different from how they believed it to be when they initially entered it. In his book, Called To Serve, Rev. Clarke states:

> [69.] "According to the 1991 *Survey of Pastors* conducted by the Fuller Institute of Church Growth, ninety per cent of pastors work more than 46 hours a week. Eighty per cent believe that pastoral ministry affects their families negatively. Thirty-three per cent said that being in ministry was an outright hazard to their families. Fifty per cent feel unable to meet the needs of the job. Seventy per cent say that they have lower self esteem now than when they started out. Forty per cent reported a serious conflict with a parishioner at least once a month. Thirty per cent confessed to having been involved in inappropriate sexual behavior with someone

in the church and seventy per cent do not have someone they consider a close friend.

These are alarming and sobering statistics that should cause anyone to think twice before making the commitment to enter the Christian ministry. For the vast majority of those who quit within five years, it is often because they simply didn't count the cost and the sacrifice that ministry would entail. Many saw glamorous preachers and evangelists on the television, others visited churches with large, vibrant congregations with impressive multimedia ministry and decide that's what they wanted to head up. Of course what they failed to realize was that which they saw was the result of years of struggle and sacrifice."

The author states that a Christian Minister is different from someone who has joined the Police Force or is enlisted in the military, neither is it like becoming a doctor, a lawyer or an aristocrat. A minister of the gospel is not a vocation, but instead, it is a "calling." When God calls someone He is literally entrusting the gospel to him or her, so the ministry does not belong to that individual, but to God. It is indeed necessary to distinguish between a profession and a calling, one chooses a profession, but God chooses those whom He wants to accomplish His purpose. A profession then, is something one is trained or taught to perform, while a calling is not just something you are taught, but it is something that you are anointed to carry out.

In olden days men of God were fearful because they were aware of the earnest responsibility the call carried. God's call is the highest call, it surpasses all other undertakings. The ancient prophets were aware that God, their Creator called them and not a human. God's call is a holy one and those who are called are to live holy. God assists those whom He calls, so that they can fulfill their assignments.

God's call is personal and no one can answer for the one who is called. Jesus laid down His life for humanity the ones who are called have to carry their own cross; they have to deny themselves and follow Jesus. The called ones have to live honest moral lives, with a willingness to stand up for the truth regardless of the outcome. God is love and we are called to love even those who hate us and abuse us.

As God calls people in the ministry, He calls them to serve. God calls a servant, as Jesus was a servant, but nowadays some ministers do not serve, they require others to serve them. They become lords and kings instead of servants of God's people.

God calls and when He does, He expects a response. He expects a reply or an action. The author alludes to a new born baby who needs to respond to the awareness of life. While the baby remained in the womb, he or she is silent, but as he or she is delivered there ought to be a sound. If the baby does not make a voluntary sound, the attending nurse or physician slaps the baby's bottom and the live baby gives out a scream. A baby who does not respond is either dead or dysfunctional. The unbeliever is unable to answer God's call because he or she is spiritually dead, there will be no life in the unsaved until God quickens him or her. After the Holy Spirit quickens and saves him or her, then that individual is alive to answer His call. God expects the Christian to answer to Him and not to anything or anyone else. The Christian who answers God first is entering in the process to Christian maturity.

Christians are to learn from Samuel who is a perfect example of one who responds promptly. He was young and lived in the temple under the supervision of the High Priest, Eli. He was sleeping near the Ark of the Covenant one night when God called him. He rose up and went to his guardian Eli, who explained to him that he did not call him and he should return to his bed. Rev. Clarke continues:

> [70.] "This is very important for all who are seeking to ascend into the ministry of the Lord. You must be willing to serve and

be led before you are ready to lead and be served. Today many want a fast track route to ministry that excludes the years of serving alongside someone else. Eli was not even a righteous leader, as we later discover in the text, but still God allowed Samuel to serve his internship with him. This, I believe is because God recognizes the importance of serving under others whatever our opinions of them might be.

Another thing to notice here is that Samuel was sleeping in the Temple beside the Ark of the Covenant, which was the very symbol of the presence of Yahweh. He desired to dwell in the very presence of God. This indicates the importance of seeking and dwelling in God's presence if we desire Him to speak to us concerning our ministry and calling. It was out of this intimacy that God called Samuel by name. He received a personal call. Whenever God is going to use us for His purpose, He will call us personally. It is good to have confirmation through word of knowledge and prophecies given by others but they are all secondary to your personal and direct call by God. The ministry is a challenging and often lonely place to be with a very high mortality rate; when the pressure is truly on you need to know beyond a shadow of a doubt that it was God who called you."

The author went on to state that during the time of Samuel's call to ministry, Israel was in such a state of apostasy that little Samuel—who wouldn't have been older than fifteen years—had never heard or witnessed God speaking to the priest or clergy. The only voice he grew to recognize was that of the 'old man' Eli, who no doubt often called him in the night with various needs.

It was time for Samuel to distinguish between two voices, the voice of his guardian, and the voice of God. Later on God appeared to Samuel, so that he was able to know God for himself, and to trust and obey God. As soon as God is ready to use us, He makes us aware of His voice over all the other voices and distractions. Samuel had to listen to what God had to say, then he had to relay the very sad message to Eli, his guardian and mentor. That message was not easy for Samuel to deliver, but in the end he had to do so. Although Samuel was a teenager he chose to obey God rather than being fearful of his senior Eli, he did not compromise God's instruction. Samuel was very obedient to God and that paid a hefty dividend, he remained faithful to God until he died; an old man. We are to be faithful to God in spite of the future.

When Jesus performed the miracle of turning water into wine, there had to be obedience on the part of the servants. Jesus, His mother, and friends were at a wedding and the wine finished as the party got more enjoyable. Mary knew that her Son could do something spectacular to save the master of the wedding from suffering embarrassment, and disgrace for years to come; he would make the headline news of our day. Mary instructed the servants to do as Jesus told them, and after they had obeyed Him, there was wine of a quality that surpassed the first batch. All Jesus did was tell them to fill the water-pots and then pour out. The master had to conclude that the best wine was saved for the last.

Steve Saint

Steve Saint, son of the famous Nate Saint, who was martyred along with four other young missionaries to South America was asked where he was a missionary, after he stated that he was Nate's, son. He said that he was a businessman and not a missionary, that reply brought disappointment to his inquirer. God had His hands on Steve's life although he did not know it at that time. Steve later became a missionary to the same people who had killed his dad. In his book, The Missionary Call, M. Davis Sills writes:

[71.] "Christians everywhere and of all ages recognize God's heartbeat to take the gospel to the nations and wrestle with the implications of the Great Commission in their own lives. Many ask how they can know for sure that God is calling them to missions. But the practical concerns inherent in discerning God's will about whether to join Him in missionary service usually throw us into a crisis because of the comfort-zone-exploding ramifications of surrendering to that call. Christians direct questions of such a vocation to college and seminary professors, pastors, mission agencies, missionaries, and friends. They ask what exactly constitutes a missionary call, how detailed it must be, and how God communicates such a call to His children. Many wonder whether a specific and personal call is necessary since it seems to them that all Christians are called and the obedient respond. Even if they are certain of a personal call to missions, they are still left with the dilemma of discovering the elusive details of where, when, how, and with whom the calling is to be fulfilled. Some who believe they are called to missions struggle with how they can follow God's calling when their spouse does not yet feel called. Confusion abounds for most believers about the missionary call."

The Word of God speaks of missions from the beginning to the end. God speaks to us through His Word so that many know Him and make Him known. He instructs us to go into "all the world," to every nation, and broadcast His glory until they too declare Him. It is safe to say that all Christians are missionaries. Steve stated that he heard a definition of a missionary as, "someone who never gets accustomed to hearing the footsteps of the heathen going to a Christless eternity."

The Scripture speaks of us being called to salvation, called to serve the Lord, and to other special duty. There are many missionaries who can say that they were certain that when the Lord called them, He called them for a definite service. There are several future missionaries who are serving the Lord in different capacities such as Sunday school Teachers, Deacons, and Lay Leaders, but become surprised when the Lord calls them to missions. Our loving God has called all Christians to salvation, holiness, discipleship and service. There are Christians who honestly struggle with the missionary call, but in the end they discover that God has called them to remain where they are and serve there; yet there are others who the call will not leave them, they have to go to the mission field. M. David Sills continues to share:

[72.] "Jesus gave us the command, the church as the missionary force, and promise that He would be with us in the fulfillment of it. His Great Commission is similar to Joshua's marching orders. After the forty years of wandering in the wilderness, God revealed to Moses he was not going into the Promised Land and told him to appoint Joshua as the next leader of Israel. Joshua's commission was to lead the people across the Jordan into

Canaan and conquer the land. In Joshua
13:1, the Lord spoke to Joshua "You are old
and advanced in years, and there remains yet
very much land to possess." God gave him
the command, Israel for an army, and His
promise to be with him in the fulfilling of the
commission. Israel was not then and is not
today a large country. With God's blessings,
one wonders why Joshua could not have
accomplished what God told him to do in
the course of his lifetime. Before we judge too
harshly, we should remember that we have
had our commission for 2,000 years, and
much of "the land" remains to be possessed.

Some might say that this is not a fair
comparison and the reason that we have not
finished the Great Commission is because we
live in a gospel-hostile world where there are
many countries to reach. Furthermore, we are
few in comparison with the religions of the
world. However, it is hard to imagine why we
still have not reached one-third of the people
in our world with the gospel. In 1896, in
Atlanta, Georgia, a man was working in his
laboratory mixing together water, flavoring,
and sugar. He invented a drink that he called
Coca-Cola. It cost him about $70 to develop
and market his product that first year and he
only made about $50. To be $20 in the red in
1896 was a tough financial loss. Nonetheless,
he continued to sell his product. A few years
later they developed a process to bottle the
drink so that people could enjoy it at home
or on picnics and the popularity grew. Today,
112 years later, 94% of the people of the world

recognize Coca-Cola logo and product.[3] In 112 years, we can reach the world for profits sake, but we cannot do it for the glory of God in 2,000 years. The keen awareness of the commands of Christ to take the gospel message to the world and our failure to do so are key components of the missionary call for many. Christ's Great Commission is for the church to be involved in reaching and teaching the nations. Every believer is to pray for the nations and support the cause of the missions, but not every believer is called to leave his homeland and go overseas. Some will help send and support, and others will go and tell."

Many Christians are saddened by the lives of the billions who have never heard the gospel, and it has become a burden to think of these unsaved loved ones who are dying without Christ. Christians are troubled with the cries of those who are born into sin every hour, live in darkness, and die in darkness. There is a great concern for those young children who are sold into sexual slavery by their own parents so that they can provide for the family. They are concerned for the street children who are sometimes hopeless. Because of these concerns they wonder how is it possible to fulfill the Great Commission if they do not assist.

God is calling people to the mission who are aware of the needs of the nations and cognizant of Christ's instructions. These are they who are affected by the needs that they observe, and are determined to do whatever the Lord bids them to do. There is no doubt about following Jesus, because these believers have a yearning desire to make His name praised and known around the world. These Christians are desirous of living a holy life for God's glory, and they know that it will require self-denial living for the lost nations of the world, so that they too can become children of God. As soon as God calls His beloved child to live the life of a missionary, He bestows upon him or her the desire with the calling. Mr. Sills further continues:

[73.] "In addition, the Lord gives a spiritual gift to every true believer (1 Corinthians 12). However, in addition to the gift itself, I believe that each believer has a passion area for the exercise of his gift. A young man may have the gift of teaching and find great freedom and affirmation as he teaches young adults. Yet, when he has the opportunity to teach preschool children or senior adults, he finds this expression of his gifts taxing and tedious. In the same way, for instance, someone could thoroughly enjoy the evangelism opportunities of international contexts much more than going on cold calls during Tuesday evening outreach at church.

Psalm 37:4 says, "Delight yourself in the LORD, and He will give you the desires of your heart." I think that this verse teaches at least two important truths. One is that the source of the desires in the heart of a person who is delighting himself in the Lord is God Himself. When we are delighting ourselves in Him, He places desires in our hearts that He wants to fulfill. When our hearts are right, He guides us by giving us godly desires. The second truth is that God gave us the desire because He wants to fulfill it. So, one can legitimately say that God guides us by our desires when we are delighting in Him. Of course, a person who is delighting himself in sin cannot claim this verse. Therefore, in discerning this missionary call, the question is often, "What do you desire to do?"

While a passionate desire and commitment to be a missionary is an indicator of God's guidance in that direction, a true call will have other markers. The believers in your home church should also see God's leading in your life. A passionate desire and commitment to serve overseas may be present for other reasons. Godly counsel and discernment is needed to know God's will."

The Bible does not define the missionary call, but it allows us to see God's desire for nations and how He calls people to Himself to carry out the desires of His heart. As we grow to know God more we can see from His Word the need for us to spread the Good News. When we think about missions we gravitate towards the New Testament to learn more about it. Acts of the Apostles, and the four gospels are prime areas that talk about missions. Revelation tells us of the great multitude from all tongues, nations, and people who will be standing before the throne and the Lamb. It also states that that great throng cannot be numbered. Although we are satisfied to say that God's call to missions is in the New Testament, we can also find where God is concerned about the people of the world in the Old Testament.

The first Preacher of the Good News to man, after the fall was God Himself. After Adam and Eve sinned, they hid from the Lord instead of running to Him, but a merciful God went looking for His children with whom He used to fellowship. God told Adam and Eve that he would place hostility between the serpent and the woman, and between her offspring and the serpent; he will bruise the head of the serpent and the serpent will bruise his heel. God promised that the seed of the woman would overcome the serpent and all his tricks.

After the fall men and women continued to sin, God brought a flood upon the earth, and destroyed women, men and animals sparing Noah, his family and some chosen animals. Sin continued after the flood, the human race continued to rebel against God, and although He extended His mercy man did not change. Man began to build a tower to reach close to heaven to worship what they perceive to be god. This perceived god was not Jehovah God. To thwart their plan, God brought changes to their language. As a result, they had difficulty communicating with each other, so they had to cease building the Tower of Babel.

We then observe God calling a man named Abram, instructing him to leave his family and country and travel to a land that He would give him. God told him that wherever his feet trod would be his. His family would also be as the stars of heaven or as the sand of the seashore which cannot be numbered. God desired that the people of the Old Testament bring glory to Him. He desires all nations to worship Him in order to bring glory to Him. Steve said that Missions is not God's goal for His people, but worship is, and mission exists because worship does not.

God called people in the Old Testament. He called them to Himself and also for a specific task. He did not give Abram a specific duty, He only gave him a command to go; and He would bless him. He called Moses to deliver the children of Israel out of bondage. He called judges and prophets whom He gave specific instructions.

God calls people in the New Testament especially to salvation. God's call can be for salvation, missions, to the ministry, to holiness, for some specific service, and to live peaceably with other men. Jesus called some of His disciples and instructed them to "follow" Him. He also told them to follow Him and He would make them "fishers of men."

CHAPTER TEN

CALLED TO SHOW MERCY

After the New Testament was written, leaders began to draw their own conclusion about God, stating that the God of the Old Testament was completely different from the God of the New Testament. Some leaders rejected the Old Testament because they believed that it had nothing to do with the gospel of Jesus. Christians believe that in the Old Testament period, God worked according to the law of demand, but operates according to the law of mercy in the New Testament. On the contrary, God is a God of grace and mercy.

The prophet Obadiah wrote about Israel being taken into exile, and instead of his brother Edom showing mercy to him, Edom assisted the enemies to bring about more burden on Israel. This caught God's attention:

> [11] For you deserted your relatives in Israel during their time of greatest need. You stood aloof, refusing to lift a finger to help when foreign invaders carried off their wealth and cast lots to divide up Jerusalem. You acted as though you were one of Israel's enemies.
>
> [12] "You shouldn't have done this! You shouldn't have gloated when they exiled your relatives to distant lands. You shouldn't have rejoiced because they were suffering such misfortune. You shouldn't have crowed over them as they suffered these disasters.

[13] You shouldn't have plundered the land of Israel when they were suffering such calamity. You shouldn't have gloated over the destruction of your relatives, looting their homes and making yourselves rich at their expense.

[14] You shouldn't have stood at the crossroads, killing those who tried to escape. You shouldn't have captured the survivors, handing them over to their enemies in that terrible time of trouble.

[15] "The day is near when I, the LORD, will judge the godless nations! As you have done to Israel, so it will be done to you. All your evil deeds will fall back on your own heads.

[16] Just as you swallowed up my people on my holy mountain, so you and the surrounding nations will swallow the punishment I pour out on you. Yes, you nations will drink and stagger and disappear from history, as though you had never even existed. Obadiah 1:11-16 (NLT).

Since the rivalry between Jacob and Esau there exists tension between the two nations. The Edomites had no mercy on Israel. When the Israelites desired to pass through their land, enroute to the Promised Land, they refused Israel's request. Obadiah had concerns about the poor Jews who were left after the Babylonian conquest, and his prophecy proved that God cared and had mercy on His children. Although He had allowed the enemies to afflict His people, His heart was moved with compassion for them because "His mercy endures forever." The heart of God was broken over His people Israel. The Evangelical Sunday School Commentary states:

[74.] "The Edomites adopted a policy of scavenging what was left over from the spoils of war in Israel. Edom sometimes avoided Babylonian aggression, and Jeremiah 40:11 indicates that some Jews immigrated to Edom for safety. Because of this, the Edomites were confident and cocky, convinced that they were untouchable. Obadiah tells them otherwise. By failing to recognize their responsibility toward Israel, they had tempted the wrath of God.

Edom had apparently mistaken itself for Babylon or Assyria! Although the prophets proclaimed that God had used those nations to pillage Israel as punishment for its sins, Edom had received no such order. Obadiah's pronouncements against Edom is full of "should" that are contrasted with "should nots." The Edomites should have been moved to compassion by the Jews' predicament. They should not have gloated, but mourned in sackcloth and ashes. If Babylon and Assyria would be punished for their treatment of God's people (even though they were acting in accordance with God's will), how much more would Edom suffer the consequences of her inaction in the face of such Jewish suffering.

Obadiah proclaims that the day of the Lord will not miss the people of Edom. Since the Edomites had scavenged the city of Jerusalem, looting its shops and houses, God's Day would visit them as well. Although the details of Edom's fate are still

debated, history shows clearly that by the
year 312 BC they were dominated by the
Nabateans, and the Edomites were no more.
God's mercy upon His suffering people had
the final word."

Israel suffered under the harsh hands of its enemies, but God delighted
in being merciful to Israel. He promised that He would send a Deliverer
to restore His people. God showed Himself in Micah, as a warrior, a
judge, and as one who meted out punishment, but in the final analysis
He showed the shepherd's heart.

CHAPTER ELEVEN

THE FULFILLMENT OF FAITHFULNESS

There was a notable man in the New Testament by the name of Saul, who loved God, kept the law, but hated the followers of Jesus. Saul did not know Jesus, and what Jesus stood for. After Jesus' death, burial, resurrection, and ascension, Saul began to cause havoc in the church. He did not hesitate one moment before he persecuted believers in the early church. Saul was neither merciful to men nor women; he hauled them all off to Jerusalem in chains.

One day as Saul traveled with his companions towards Damascus to persecute and arrest Christians. Jesus met him on the way. Saul did not know that Jesus came to save sinners, so he hated those who proclaimed Jesus, whom he thought was dead, to be alive. I think that Saul feared what he did not know, so he was willing to destroy what was foreign to him:

> ³ As he was nearing Damascus on this mission, a brilliant light from heaven suddenly beamed down upon him!
>
> ⁴ He fell to the ground and heard a voice saying to him, "Saul! Saul! Why are you persecuting me?"
>
> ⁵ "Who are you, sir?" Saul asked. And the voice replied, "I am Jesus, the one you are persecuting!
>
> ⁶ Now get up and go into the city, and you will be told what you are to do."

⁷ The men with Saul stood speechless with surprise, for they heard the sound of someone's voice, but they saw no one!

⁸ As Saul picked himself up off the ground, he found that he was blind.

⁹ So his companions led him by the hand to Damascus. He remained there blind for three days. And all that time he went without food and water.

¹⁰ Now there was a believer in Damascus named Ananias. The Lord spoke to him in a vision, calling, "Ananias!" "Yes, Lord!" he replied.

¹¹ The Lord said, "Go over to Straight Street, to the house of Judas. When you arrive, ask for Saul of Tarsus. He is praying to me right now.

¹² I have shown him a vision of a man named Ananias coming in and laying his hands on him so that he can see again."

¹³ "But Lord," exclaimed Ananias, "I've heard about the terrible things this man has done to the believers in Jerusalem!

¹⁴ And we hear that he is authorized by the leading priests to arrest every believer in Damascus."

[15] But the Lord said, "Go and do what I say. For Saul is my chosen instrument to take my message to the Gentiles and to kings, as well as to the people of Israel.

[16] And I will show him how much he must suffer for me." Acts 9:3-16 (NLT).

After Jesus called Saul, and changed his name to Paul he was not afraid to suffer for Jesus. He represented Jesus before nobles and even royalties. If he was threatened by death, he was ready to die, if he was given life, it did not bother him.

Jesus called Paul, and he responded positively to his call. He fulfilled his call in a dignified manner. He wrote letters to churches from jail, encouraging and correcting others. He represented the Gospel in a phenomenal manner. Paul's final words to Christians are:

[6] As for me, my life has already been poured out as an offering to God. The time of my death is near.

[7] I have fought a good fight, I have finished the race, and I have remained faithful.

[8] And now the prize awaits me—the crown of righteousness that the Lord, the righteous Judge, will give me on that great day of his return. And the prize is not just for me but for all who eagerly look forward to his glorious return. II Timothy 4:7-8 (NLT).

I pray that all those who respond to God's call will end the race with the commendation that Paul used for himself.

BIBLIOGRAPHY

[1] The New Grolier Webster International Dictionary of The English Language. Volume 1: Grolier Incorporated, New York. Copyright © 1974, 1973, 1972, 1971. by The English-Language Institute of America, Inc.

[2] Redemption Songs. 1000 Hymns and Choruses, (Pickering & Inglis. London-Glasgow) p.121

[3] David Spangler, <u>The Call</u> (The Berkley Publishing Group, New York: 375 Hudson Street, 1996), pp. 13-15

[4] David Spangler, <u>The Call</u>, (The Berkley Publishing Group, New York: 375 Hudson Street, 1996), pp. 10-11.

[5] Carole Mayhall, <u>Help Lord My Whole Life Hurts</u>, (Navpress, Colorado: Colorado Springs, A Ministry of The Navigators, 1988 Second Printing 1989.) pp. 12-13.

[6] Carole Mayhall, <u>Help Lord My Whole Life Hurts</u>, (Navpress, Colorado: Colorado Springs, A Ministry of The Navigators, 1988 Second Printing 1989.) pp. 43-45.

[7] Carole Mayhall, <u>Help Lord My Whole Life Hurts</u>, (Navpress, Colorado: Colorado Springs, A Ministry of The Navigators, 1988 Second Printing 1989.) p. 62.

[8] Sarah Young, <u>Jesus Calling</u>, (Thomas Nelson, Inc., Tennessee: Nashville, 2004), p.8

[9] Sarah Young, <u>Jesus Calling</u>, (Thomas Nelson, Inc., Tennessee: Nashville, 2004), p.19

[10] Sarah Young, <u>Jesus Calling</u>, (Thomas Nelson, Inc., Tennessee: Nashville, 2004), p.83

[11] The New Grolier Webster International Dictionary of The English Language. Volume 1: Grolier Incorporated, New York. Copyright © 1974, 1973, 1972, 1971. by The English-Language Institute of America, Inc.

[12] Evangelical Sunday School Lesson Commentary. (Pathway Press, Tennessee: Cleveland, 2011-2012), p. 21.

[13] Evangelical Sunday School Lesson Commentary. (Pathway Press, Tennessee: Cleveland, 2011-2012), p. 22.

[14] Evangelical Sunday School Lesson Commentary. (Pathway Press, Tennessee: Cleveland, 2011-2012), p. 24.

[15] Michael Catt, A Call To Courageous Living, (B & H Publishing Group, Tennessee: Nashville, 2011), pp. 19-20.

[16] Michael Catt, A Call To Courageous Living, (B & H Publishing Group, Tennessee: Nashville 2011), pp. 27-28

[17] Michael Catt, A Call To Courageous Living, (B & H Publishing Group, Tennessee: Nashville 2011), pp. 43-44.

[18] Kay Arthur, The Call to Follow Jesus. (Oregon: Eugene, Harvest House Publishing, 1994), pp.15-16.

[19] Kay Arthur, The Call to Follow Jesus. (Oregon: Eugene, Harvest House Publishing, 1994), p.48.

[20] Kay Arthur, The Call to Follow Jesus. (Oregon: Eugene, Harvest House Publishing, 1994), p.60.

[21] Twila Paris with Robert Webber, In This Sanctuary, (Star Song Publishing Group, Tennessee: Nashville, 1993), p. 19.

[22] Twila Paris with Robert Webber, <u>In This Sanctuary,</u> (Star Song Publishing Group, Tennessee: Nashville, 1993), p. 21.

[23] Twila Paris with Robert Webber, <u>In This Sanctuary,</u> (Star Song Publishing Group, Tennessee: Nashville, 1993), pp. 26-27

[24] Twila Paris with Robert Webber, <u>In This Sanctuary,</u> (Star Song Publishing Group, Tennessee: Nashville, 1993), pp. 41-42.

[25] Twila Paris with Robert Webber, <u>In This Sanctuary,</u> (Star Song Publishing Group, Tennessee: Nashville, 1993), pp. 63-64.

[26] Twila Paris with Robert Webber, <u>In This Sanctuary,</u> (Star Song Publishing Group, Tennessee: Nashville, 1993), pp. 67-68.

[27] Twila Paris with Robert Webber, <u>In This Sanctuary,</u> (Star Song Publishing Group, Tennessee: Nashville, 1993), pp. 77-79.

[28] Twila Paris with Robert Webber, <u>In This Sanctuary,</u> (Star Song Publishing Group, Tennessee: Nashville, 1993), p. 86.

[29] Twila Paris with Robert Webber, <u>In This Sanctuary,</u> (Star Song Publishing Group, Tennessee: Nashville, 1993), p. 139.

[30] Gary McIntosh & Glen Martin, <u>Finding Them, Keeping Them,</u> (B & H Publishing Group, Tennessee: Nashville 1992), p13.

[31] Gary McIntosh & Glen Martin, <u>Finding Them, Keeping Them,</u> (B & H Publishing Group, Tennessee: Nashville 1992), pp.14-15.

[32] Gary McIntosh & Glen Martin, <u>Finding Them, Keeping Them,</u> (B & H Publishing Group, Tennessee: Nashville 1992), p.13.

[33] Helen K. Hosier, <u>William And Catherine Booth, Founders of The Salvation Army.</u> (Barbour Publishing, OH: Uhrichsville1979), pp. 7-9.

[34] Helen K. Hosier, <u>William And Catherine Booth, Founders of The Salvation Army</u>. (Barbour Publishing, OH: Uhrichsville1979), pp. 72-73.

[35] Helen K. Hosier, <u>William And Catherine Booth, Founders of The Salvation Army</u>. (Barbour Publishing, OH: Uhrichsville1979), pp. 94-95

[36] Helen K. Hosier, <u>William And Catherine Booth, Founders of The Salvation Army</u>. (Barbour Publishing, OH: Uhrichsville1979), p. 125

[37] Helen K. Hosier, <u>William And Catherine Booth, Founders of The Salvation Army</u>. (Barbour Publishing, OH: Uhrichsville1979), pp. 131-133.

[38] Helen K. Hosier, <u>William And Catherine Booth, Founders of The Salvation Army</u>. (Barbour Publishing, OH: Uhrichsville1979), pp. 167-168.

[39] Helen K. Hosier, <u>William And Catherine Booth, Founders of The Salvation Army</u>. (Barbour Publishing, OH: Uhrichsville1979), pp. 176-177.

[40] Helen K. Hosier, <u>William And Catherine Booth, Founders of The Salvation Army</u>. (Barbour Publishing, OH: Uhrichsville1979), p. 191.

[41] W. Terry Whalin, <u>Sojourner Truth American Abolitionist,</u> (Barbour Publishing, Inc., Ohio: Uhrichsville, MCMXCV11), pp. 16-17.

[42] W. Terry Whalin, <u>Sojourner Truth American Abolitionist,</u> (Barbour Publishing, Inc., Ohio: Uhrichsville, MCMXCV11), pp. 22-23.

[43] W. Terry Whalin, <u>Sojourner Truth American Abolitionist,</u> (Barbour Publishing, Inc., Ohio: Uhrichsville, MCMXCV11), pp. 24-25.

[44] W. Terry Whalin, <u>Sojourner Truth American Abolitionist,</u> (Barbour Publishing, Inc., Ohio: Uhrichsville, MCMXCV11), p. 28.

[45] W. Terry Whalin, <u>Sojourner Truth American Abolitionist,</u> (Barbour Publishing, Inc., Ohio: Uhrichsville, MCMXCV11), pp. 35-36

[46] W. Terry Whalin, <u>Sojourner Truth American Abolitionist,</u> (Barbour Publishing, Inc., Ohio: Uhrichsville, MCMXCV11), pp. 42-43

[47] W. Terry Whalin, <u>Sojourner Truth American Abolitionist,</u> (Barbour Publishing, Inc., Ohio: Uhrichsville, MCMXCV11), p. 101.

[48] W. Terry Whalin, <u>Sojourner Truth American Abolitionist,</u> (Barbour Publishing, Inc., Ohio: Uhrichsville, MCMXCV11), p. 158

[49] W. Terry Whalin, <u>Sojourner Truth American Abolitionist,</u> (Barbour Publishing, Inc., Ohio: Uhrichsville, MCMXCV11), pp. 161-162.

[50] W. Terry Whalin, <u>Sojourner Truth American Abolitionist,</u> (Barbour Publishing, Inc., Ohio: Uhrichsville, MCMXCV11), pp. 169-170.

[51] Basil Miller, <u>George Muller, Man Of Faith And Miracles</u>. (Bethany House Publishers, Minnesota: Minneapolis, Zonderman Publishing House), 1941, pp. 7-8.

[52] Basil Miller, <u>George Muller, Man Of Faith And Miracles</u>. (Bethany House Publishers, Minnesota: Minneapolis, Zonderman Publishing House), 1941, pp. 11-12.

[53] Basil Miller, <u>George Muller, Man Of Faith And Miracles</u>. (Bethany House Publishers, Minnesota: Minneapolis, Zonderman Publishing House), 1941, pp. 15-16.

[54] Basil Miller, <u>George Muller, Man Of Faith And Miracles</u>. (Bethany House Publishers, Minnesota: Minneapolis, Zonderman Publishing House), 1941, p. 20.

[55] Basil Miller, <u>George Muller, Man Of Faith And Miracles</u>. (Bethany House Publishers, Minnesota: Minneapolis, Zonderman Publishing House), 1941, pp. 28-30.

[56] Basil Miller, <u>George Muller, Man Of Faith And Miracles</u>. (Bethany House Publishers, Minnesota: Minneapolis, Zonderman Publishing House), 1941, p. 126.

[57] Sam Wellman, <u>Gladys Aylward, Missionary To China,</u> (Barbour Publishing, OH: Uhrichsville, MCMXCV11), pp. 10-12.

[58] Sam Wellman, <u>Gladys Aylward, Missionary To China,</u> (Barbour Publishing, OH: Uhrichsville, MCMXCV11), pp. 25-26.

[59] Sam Wellman, <u>Gladys Aylward, Missionary To China,</u> (Barbour Publishing, OH: Uhrichsville, MCMXCV11), pp. 28-29.

[60] Sam Wellman, <u>Gladys Aylward, Missionary To China,</u> (Barbour Publishing, OH: Uhrichsville, MCMXCV11), pp. 51-52.

[61] Sam Wellman, <u>Gladys Aylward, Missionary To China,</u> (Barbour Publishing, OH: Uhrichsville, MCMXCV11), pp. 65-66.

[62] Sam Wellman, <u>Gladys Aylward, Missionary To China,</u> (Barbour Publishing, OH: Uhrichsville, MCMXCV11), pp. 187-188.

[63] Sam Wellman, <u>Gladys Aylward, Missionary To China,</u> (Barbour Publishing, OH: Uhrichsville, MCMXCV11), pp. 201-202.

[64] Collie Smith Grant, <u>Free Indeed, African-American Christians and the Struggle for Equality</u>. James W.C. Pennington. <u>Harriet Tubman.</u> Mary McLeod Bethune. Rosa Parks (Barbour Publishing Inc., Ohio: Uhrichsville, 2003), pp. 67-68.

[65] Collie Smith Grant, <u>Free Indeed, African-American Christians and the Struggle for Equality</u>. James W.C. Pennington. <u>Harriet</u>

Tubman. Mary McLeod Bethune. Rosa Parks (Barbour Publishing Inc., Ohio: Uhrichsville, 2003), p. 71.

[66] Collie Smith Grant, Free Indeed, African-American Christians and the Struggle for Equality. James W.C. Pennington. Harriet Tubman. Mary McLeod Bethune. Rosa Parks (Barbour Publishing Inc., Ohio: Uhrichsville, 2003), pp. 91-92.

[67] Collie Smith Grant, Free Indeed, African-American Christians and the Struggle for Equality. James W.C. Pennington. Harriet Tubman. Mary McLeod Bethune. Rosa Parks (Barbour Publishing Inc., Ohio: Uhrichsville, 2003), pp. 99-100.

[68] Collie Smith Grant, Free Indeed, African-American Christians and the Struggle for Equality. James W.C. Pennington. Harriet Tubman. Mary McLeod Bethune. Rosa Parks (Barbour Publishing Inc., Ohio: Uhrichsville, 2003), pp. 105-107.

[69] Clifton R. Clarke, Called To Serve, (Step Publishers, Ghana: Accra-North, 2007), pp. 19-20.

[70] Clifton R. Clarke, Called To Serve, (Step Publishers, Ghana: Accra-North, 2007), pp. 30-32.

[71] M. David Sills, The Missionary Call, (Moody Publishers, IL: Chicago, 2008), pp. 13-14.

[72] M. David Sills, The Missionary Call, (Moody Publishers, IL: Chicago, 2008), pp. 24-25.

[73] M. David Sills, The Missionary Call, (Moody Publishers, IL: Chicago, 2008), pp. 27-28.

[74] Evangelical Sunday School Lesson Commentary. (Pathway Press, Tennessee: Cleveland, 2011-2012), pp. 49-50.